Making It in Real Estate

Starting Out as a Developer

John McNellis

Urban Land Institute
Leadership Network

About the Urban Land Institute

The mission of the Urban Land Institute is to provide leadership in the responsible use of land and in creating and sustaining thriving communities worldwide. ULI is committed to

- Bringing together leaders from across the fields of real estate and land use policy to exchange best practices and serve community needs;
- Fostering collaboration within and beyond ULI's membership through mentoring, dialogue, and problem solving;
- Exploring issues of urbanization, conservation, regeneration, land use, capital formation, and sustainable development;
- Advancing land use policies and design practices that respect the uniqueness of both built and natural environments;
- Sharing knowledge through education, applied research, publishing, and electronic media; and
- Sustaining a diverse global network of local practice and advisory efforts that address current and future challenges.

Established in 1936, the Institute today has more than 38,000 members representing the entire spectrum of the land use and development disciplines. ULI relies heavily on the experience of its members. It is through member involvement and information resources that ULI has been able to set standards of excellence in development practice. The Institute has long been recognized as one of the world's most respected and widely quoted sources of objective information on urban planning, growth, and development.

Patrick L. Phillips, Global Chief Executive Officer, ULI

©2016 Urban Land Institute
2001 L Street NW, Suite 200
Washington, DC 20036

Recommended bibliographic listing:
McNellis, John. *Making It in Real Estate: Starting Out as a Developer.* Washington, D.C.: Urban Land Institute, 2016.

ISBN: 978-0-87420-383-7

About the Author

John McNellis is a principal with McNellis Partners, a commercial development firm he cofounded in the mid-1980s in northern California. After graduating from the University of California, Berkeley, and the University of California Hastings College of the Law, McNellis began his career as a lawyer in 1976 in San Francisco. Always more interested in business than in law, he started fixing up houses in his spare time and gradually worked his way to more complicated projects. At 28, he formed a partnership with an older client and began his career as a retail developer. Cobbling together the equity from friends and family, they built and opened their first shopping center in 1983, by which time McNellis was no longer practicing law—except on behalf of his own projects. Within a few years, he formed McNellis Partners with Beth Walter and Mike Powers. They continue to be partners more than 30 years later. Specializing in developing supermarket-anchored shopping centers in northern California, the partnership has followed a strategy of developing only about two projects a year and doing so with internal capital only, thus retaining 100 percent ownership of their developments. In recent years, the company has begun developing mixed-use projects and, in an effort to diversify, investing in small Silicon Valley office buildings.

ULI Project Staff

Jeanne Myerson
Chief Executive Officer, Americas

Dean Schwanke
Senior Vice President
Case Studies and Publications

Ellen Mendelsohn
Director
ULI Leadership Network

David Mulvihill
Vice President, Professional
Development Programs

James A. Mulligan
Senior Editor

Marcy Gessel, Publications Professionals LLC
Manuscript Editor

Betsy Van Buskirk
Creative Director

Deanna Pineda, Muse Advertising Design
Graphic Design

Craig Chapman
Senior Director, Publishing Operations

About the ULI Leadership Network

The ULI Leadership Network seeks to cultivate the professional and personal growth of its members, thereby enhancing their organizations and communities, the industry, and the built environment. The Leadership Network uses interdisciplinary engagement to provide exposure to varied viewpoints and multiple stakeholders. It fosters relationships, facilitates industry collaboration, imparts knowledge, and prepares members to become leaders at multiple professional levels and as individual influencers within their communities.

The Leadership Network connects ULI members to opportunities throughout the organization in which they can both learn and make an impact during the span of their career. In addition to these efforts, the Leadership Network operates seven programs:

- Larson Leadership Initiative
- Women's Leadership Initiative
- ULI NEXT Global
- Centers for Leadership
- UrbanPlan
- Professional Development
- Scholarships and Student Fellowships

Contents

Preface

I LEARNED REAL ESTATE as I had learned the facts of life. On the street. I learned development gradually—deal by deal—often acquiring experience just after I needed it. Had there been a practical book on development when I started out, I would have read it because, while we sometimes appear doomed to make our own mistakes, we do occasionally remember the advice of others and spare ourselves the first-degree burns our own inexperience would have failed to prevent.

That is why I've written this book.

As complex and risky as real estate development is—an encyclopedia rather than a primer would be required to cover all a developer should know—there are certain truths so obvious they can be book-learned. If they are not, lessons will be learned the hard way, the expensive way, usually at the very moment the fledgling developer realizes she's too far out over her ski tips.

In this book, I ask you to consider whether you truly wish to leave the comfort and security of your salaried position and whether you—and your family—might not be better off if you were to pursue your desire to develop on the side. I have no statistics on this, but a career's worth of observation and anecdotal evidence have taught me that a considerable majority of developers might have been far better off, financially and emotionally, limiting their real estate pursuits to an avocation.

The true developers among you will brush aside this advice as meant for others. And it is for you—the true developer—that I offer what I trust will be useful advice on everything from what you should buy to how you should focus your objectives to running your own firm to dealing with the players in our world: the bankers, partners, politicians, consultants, and brokers. If there is an overarching theme in these pages, it is simply this: the best way to survive, and thrive, is to manage every risk within your control. So many risks are beyond your control—interest rates, global tectonic shifts, the bankruptcies of your tenants, even the weather—you will, like the rest of us, invariably lose money one day. Whether that loss proves a temporary setback or the end of your career may depend on how you have managed your other risks. If you have created firewalls by limiting your exposure to your lenders, partners, vendors, and service providers, you will survive. If, however, your first loss is the domino that causes your other risks to tumble, you may not.

My desire, then, is to leave you holding the same admiration, caution, and healthy respect for real estate development that a zookeeper has for his lions.

Making It in Real Estate
Starting Out as a Developer

John McNellis

Quit Your Job?

OVER A BEER, A YOUNG FRIEND RECOUNTED his progress with a retail development firm. I was surprised to hear how much he had learned and how much responsibility he already had. When he explained his lead role on a mixed-use project, I asked how profitable the development would be for the company. He guessed about $10 million. I asked if he had a profit share. Reluctantly, he explained that he had been promised a percentage in the deal but that his employer, a man of infinite wealth, had gone silent on the issue. With nothing in writing and the project's final entitlements days away, he could only hope his boss would honor his word.

It could be that this jillionaire simply has a lot on his mind—which jet to use for the St. Tropez trip can be a consuming decision—or it could be that no amount of wealth will ever make him do the right thing.

Business has few certainties, but one is this: employees are seldom paid more than "go money." That is, companies large and small, public and private, will pay enough to keep their key employees from going elsewhere. The publics blame their parsimony on their duty to their shareholders, and the privates blame their silent but surprisingly stingy partners.

If your dissatisfaction is with the job itself—and not your income— you should quit. That is, if you can afford the cash flow hit. If you're an entrepreneur at heart and the only decision you're making at work is where to park in the morning, quit. If you can cobble together a year's worth of living expenses and go into business and fail, what's your downside? Merely the salary loss from your crappy job. And if you have to white-flag it back to the corporate world, you will be more valuable because of your experience. Potential employers will know you are ambitious, that you have an owner's perspective, and that—let's face it—you're unlikely to bolt again.

It's a different story if it's all about the money. If you love your job and your hunger is only for wealth, then ask yourself when you're sober—or better yet, badly hung over—if you're really worth more than go money. If you still think so, explain to your boss how valuable you are, ask for a big raise, and then listen hard to the reply. He's your boss for a reason. He has more experience than you do, and it's even theoretically possible that he is smarter than you or at least a tad better in business (these are two entirely different things: many of the smartest people I know are terrible at business). And if your boss says your compensation is fair, he may be right. In my experience, those who start a business just to get rich almost never succeed. The ones who make it are those who love what they're doing and start their own companies only because they have no choice (no one will hire them), because they want to be their own boss, or because they think they can do it better on their own. They believe they will be more productive—and have more fun—if they can peel away the corporate bureaucracy, the weekly team conference calls, the Sisyphean reporting requirements, the multiple sign-offs needed for deals, and even the mandatory company socializing.

I asked George Marcus, one of the most successful men in American real estate, what he thought about starting a company for the money. "Anyone dreaming of going into business just to get rich is fooling himself. You start a business because you have a passion to improve a business strategy or an industry." George knows what he's talking about. At 25, he started Marcus & Millichap and finally took it public in 2013 (the stock price has since doubled). He is also the founder and principal shareholder of another public company, Essex Property Trust, arguably the country's best-performing real estate investment trust over the past 20 years.

Mervin Morris, a giant in the retail industry and founder of the Mervyn's department store chain, told me simply, "I went into business for myself because I wanted to be my own boss and make a comfortable living." Personally, I switched from real estate law to development because it seemed to me that developers have a lot more fun than lawyers do (I was right). My sole financial ambition at the time was to make as much as a developer as I would have as a lawyer.

Turning Gordon Gekko's aphorism on its head, greed is not good enough.

Where does all this leave my young friend who loves his job and its challenges but who will likely end up unhappy with his compensation? (By the way, if you can succeed at running your own business, you will always be unhappy with your compensation.) If, like George, he thinks he can do it better on his own or, like Merv, he wants to be his own boss, or if he simply wants to have more fun, then he should consider setting up shop.

But to paraphrase the teachings of Siddhartha, there is a "middle way" that we will explore in the next chapter.

Doing It on the Side

ARE WE IN THE WRONG BUSINESS?

On the "Best Jobs in America" lists, a career in real estate rates lower than carjacking. In fact, commercial real estate doesn't rate at all on these ubiquitous lists. The closest we come is "real estate agent," a distant #89 on *U.S. News & World Report's* Top 100 Jobs list, lapped by such swell careers as "substance abuse counselor" (#36), "bill collector" (#57), and "exterminator" (#61).

And at $80,000 a year, "real estate brokers" earn #159 among the Top 300 Highest Paying Jobs published by Myplan.com. That list's top 20 paying jobs, by the way, are all physicians, starting with anesthesiologists at $233,000 and ending with general practitioners at $181,000.

Should we be applying to med school, or is it possible these data don't tell the whole story? Misreading data is a common failing—"Son, you got four F's and a D. What's that tell you?" the father asks. "That I'm spending too much time on one subject, Daddy?" To deduce that one should elect a career in exterminating rather than real estate courtesy of *U.S. News* is likely such a mistake.

What best-jobs data will never reveal is one of real estate's greatest strengths—that is, that one can amass a considerable fortune by doing it on the side. What other part-time work or avocation is so lucrative? You could probably work part time as an exterminator or perhaps even as an anesthesiologist, but as long as you are working by the hour—as long as you're working and your capital isn't—you will be stuck in the economic middle class.

If you love your day job but are unhappy with its compensation—the dilemma posed in chapter 1—you don't have to quit. You just need to start a new hobby: give up fantasy football and while away your free time on a dilapidated house. And if you take the long view—you should, real estate is the classic get-rich-slow business—you will do well.

My late father-in-law was a bright man who came home from World War II devastated by his experiences as a combat medic in the South Pacific. As with many veterans, Bill found solace in the bottle, and by the time he was in his mid-30s he was an alcoholic—drinking a six-pack of beer and a bottle of vodka every day. Yet Bill somehow found the fortitude to quit drinking and start life over at 45. With no savings, no formal education beyond high school, and no marketable skills other than a talent for sales, Bill slowly amassed a small collection of San Francisco Bay Area real estate—a couple of houses, a few promissory notes, a duplex or two, and a five-unit building— worth several million dollars at the time of his death 40 years later. More important, his real estate allowed him to retire in his late 60s with a secure income of $150,000 a year.

How did he do it? One small building at a time. Bill made his living by day but his fortune by night, buying a property every year or two, fixing it up, sometimes selling it, sometimes keeping it. His properties were never pretty— they probably lost money at first—but 25 years later when it was time to retire, he had paid off their mortgages and his cash flow was as free and clear as a Sierra stream.

And it's really that simple.

If you love your job or find the prospect of going out on your own—of working without a net—overwhelming, and yet you still want a future independent of a corporate pension, buy a neglected house in a quiet town and get started. If you can cobble together enough of a down payment—perhaps with family and friends' money (the topic of a later chapter)—so that you at least break even after paying your expenses, you're set. Even if your rents never increase a cent, you will eventually pay off the mortgage and all that cash flow will be yours. If you can pull this off a few times, you can retire as comfortably as my father-in-law did.

Playing Small Ball

"I HIT BIG OR I MISS BIG. I like to live as big as I can." A winning formula for the greatest baseball player ever, but unless you're determined to become real estate's Babe Ruth, you might consider following in someone else's spikes. Mortals make the Hall of Fame by hitting singles. The late Tony Gwynn was dearly remembered as a better person than a hitter, and he was the greatest hitter of his generation. Tony hit singles. Derek Jeter will make the Hall hitting singles.

And so can you. But this is where the baseball metaphor strikes out—players make the Hall of Fame batting .300. You won't. Unless you're making money on eight out of every ten deals, you'll enter a different hall, the one where you file Chapter 11.

Don Kuemmeler, a founding partner of Pacific Coast Capital Partners, is more precise. Don says PCCP, a $6.5 billion real estate management firm, has to bat .850 on its equity deals and .990 on its debt placements to maintain its targeted profitability.

How should you choose real estate investments? The same way you take a lion's temperature—very carefully. Hitting those numbers isn't easy—

$6.5 billion firms are few and far between for a reason—because sooner or later, everyone loses money in real estate.

Even when you are careful you will hit a rough patch (especially if you persist in thinking of a second home as an investment). If you bought anything in the 2004–2007 bubble, you lost big. But this is the point: if you didn't have to sell, your losses were merely on paper. And if you could afford to wait long enough, you actually turned a profit. If, however, you were forced to sell bubble-era acquisitions in 2009–2011, you lost, somewhere between a lot and everything. What three factors force one to sell into a terrible market? Debt, debt, and debt. The other "D's"—death, divorce, and disaster—are far easier to ignore than a foreclosure notice nailed to your door.

In baseball, the difference between a single and a home run is how hard you swing the bat; in real estate, it's how much leverage you use.

In a rising market, leverage turns singles into home runs. Let's say you bought a $5 million property with a million dollars in equity and a $4 million loan and that two years later it's worth $6 million. You would have achieved a 100 percent return on your million-dollar investment. Home run. If you had instead purchased the same property with no debt, your return would be 20 percent (a million dollar profit on a $5 million cash investment). Single.

Note that we're simply measuring the return on your equity investment to determine your level of success.

If, however, the property had lost 20 percent of its value, the leveraged buyer would be tapioca—the equity gone and the property too when the loan matures. On the other hand, the cash buyer has a 20 percent loss on paper, but nothing else changes. Assuming the drop in value is systemic (e.g., the Great Recession), the property's cash flow remains the same: if you were making $300,000 a year when the property was worth $5 million, you're still making $300,000 when it's worth $4 million. Bob Hughes, one of the most original thinkers in our business, drawled in the depths of the recession, "John, my net worth's gone down by half, but my cash flow's the same." And since net worth is meaningless (see chapter 17), since ultimately it's all about cash flow, nothing changed for the talented Mr. Hughes. Nor will it for you if you are prudent with leverage.

It's hard to hit a home run paying all cash, but it's also impossible to strike out, and since even the best in our business lose money, you might seriously consider small ball. By the way, the Bambino himself agreed with this philosophy: "If I'd tried for them dinking singles, I could've batted around .800." And so can you.

Finally, if you're truly going out on your own, take this last bit of advice from the Babe to heart: "Never let the fear of striking out get in your way."

Specialize or Die

A RECENT COLLEGE GRADUATE WROTE, asking for advice. Mentioning how thrilled he was to be accepted into Marcus & Millichap's training program, he wanted to know which area he should specialize in: land, apartments, or industrial. I told him it didn't matter as long as he picked one and stuck with it. Yet to spend his first day in real estate, this fellow had already figured out a truth that eludes many: if you don't specialize, your specialty will be failure.

In small towns noted more for alfalfa than economic opportunities, a broker can be a grammar school teacher—that is, he can know just enough about half a dozen subjects to be one step ahead of his clients and sell anything that walks in the door, from ranches to diners to mobile homes. In a city of size, the competent broker is more of a high school teacher, sticking with one broad subject, selling, say, only industrial properties. And in major markets, top brokers are more akin to university professors, focusing on narrow niches within their specialty—an office leasing agent who represents only law firms.

But which specialty matters little and which niche almost not at all because each product type will have its days in the sun over the years. What you do doesn't matter that much, but where you do it is huge. To paraphrase

Warren Buffett, I'd rather be a mediocre developer in a brilliant city than a brilliant developer in Lancaster, California. My advice? If you're stuck in my hometown or any other city with Lancaster's dim prospects, move.

Like every other clueless neophyte, we started out in apartments, but, as profitable as they are for many, they didn't work for us. Richer in experience but little else, we soon decided we had no wish to own buildings where anyone slept. Waving farewell to our tenants—some of whom were arguably sane—we shifted into the fast lane, the glamour world of suburban industrial. How hard could industrial be, we asked ourselves. Within months of buying our first pair of warehouses, we began learning about our new business (experience is something you acquire just after you need it). It belatedly dawned on us that when the biggest player in town not only owns a Pangaea of free land but a construction company that must be kept busy, he is going to stop building warehouses the week after we rescind the Louisiana Purchase. And rents are never going to rise. Ten years later, we cracked the Dom Perignon when we managed to sell our warehouses for exactly what we paid for them. This time we waved bye-bye to tenants who, as always, were merrily melting our parking lot with their cleaning solvents and oil changing.

In short, rather than being apartment and industrial moguls, we might have more profitably spent our time as forest fire lookouts. But all was not lost. Somewhere during our ten years in the industrial wilderness, we fell into a retail deal and developed a shopping center in Healdsburg, California. That project—we still own it—became the template for everything we've developed ever since, namely, neighborhood shopping centers in cities that fight development as if it were contagious. The degree to which we specialize is worth stressing. Within the high school subject of retail, our professor's niche is this: our development projects are "necessity retail" (supermarkets, drug stores, and discount department stores); they range from 25,000 to 150,000 square feet; and they are located within a two-hour drive of San Francisco. Within that narrow range, we can often be competitive with larger, better-known developers, challenging their superior capital with local knowledge and an ability to act quickly.

Our geographic limitation—that two-hour drive time—isn't based purely on laziness. If a project is no more than two hours away, we can drive there, have the meeting with the city, get our hats handed to us, and still get back to the office to deal with other challenges.

By the way, specializing doesn't mean that you shouldn't move on once the tin mine is played out. When it finally sputters, you need to pick a new specialty (and then stick with that) or a new area.

If you become a developer and have any success at it, you will one day receive a call from a silver-tongued broker. She will be calling from a land far away, from Atlanta or Denver or perhaps Houston. She will flatter you with blandishments about your reputation and, when at last she deems you ready, she will describe a wonderful opportunity that somehow all of the local developers in her city have managed to overlook. Before responding to her siren call, ask yourself this: how likely is it that Atlanta or Denver or Houston doesn't have even one homegrown, totally connected developer who is at least as smart as you? And then thank the broker for the call and stay home.

Bromancing the Deal

"I ALWAYS ACT AS OUR BROKER when we buy properties. That way I take the commission we save as my fee and it doesn't cost my investors anything." Except seeing good deals. In a dead heat with drunk-texting, this is among the worst mistakes a young principal can make. The problem with acting as your own broker is that it works beautifully on crap, thereby masking its insidious effect on good deals. If a broker had a listing on land in Chernobyl, she would gladly share her commission with you or Charles Manson or even Donald Trump to get rid of it. And toss in a closing dinner.

Good deals are another story.

In hot markets, great deals are rare. They're scarce even after the bubble is blown. And if the brokerage community knows you're representing yourself, you will swiftly discover where the Mafia learned its code of silence. The listing broker may begrudgingly send you her sales package, but will she share what else she knows about the property? Are you ever going to have a listing on which she will need your help? No. If, instead of insisting on half of the commission, you allow yourself to be represented by another broker, you create two potential sources of future deals instead of one agent certain you screwed her out of a full commission. Buy three deals in a year and, in scenario one, you have three brokers who won't return your calls or, in scenario two, six who think you're a stand-up guy.

For anyone meant for the business, this should be obvious. The next rung on this ladder is almost as evident: in a competitive situation, always pay the listing broker the full commission. Even if this means paying your own broker on the side. It is unlikely Einstein really said, "The most powerful force in the universe is compound interest," but if he were given to monetary ruminations, he might have added, "It's second only to the power of the financial incentive." In a hot market, the listing broker may be presenting a half dozen offers to his seller. If the offers are close, which is he going to tout? Those in which he nets $50,000 or the one in which he pockets $100,000? If your answer is anything but the latter, consider joining a Tibetan monastery.

On the other hand, money alone is not enough—it never is. Mirroring life itself, business is about relationships. In real estate, a *bromance* is your friendship with your broker (male or female), presumably platonic but deep nonetheless. Wise principals spend quality time with their favored brokers. Why? Because they are truly friends and it doesn't hurt when it comes to getting the "first call, last look" on deals.

The advice then is simple: work on your relationships, become friends with your brokers, and treat them fairly. This is not to suggest, however, that you should accept any broker's proposed commission schedule or listing agreement without first ascertaining what the going rate is. And then fighting a bit. Tasmanian devils are hamsters compared with brokers arguing over their fees.

Beyond the basics of treating agents with respect, choosing the right one matters because the best are as specialized as the best principals. The major houses with their vast marketing networks are superb at extracting a buyer's last nickel and thus brilliant if you're a seller and not—unless you have a pathological need to overpay—all that useful to buyers. The small shops tend to be where the best buy-side deals are ferreted out, usually a result of determination and local knowledge.

In retail, the best buyers' brokers are often not the investment sales guys but leasing agents. This is intuitive: retail is about tenants, about delivering the right tenant to the right location, and tenant reps know exactly where their clients want to open stores. Often enough, these agents encounter sites where the existing ownership is unwilling—or unable—to execute on development opportunities.

Once you've selected the right broker and are treating her the way you would wish to be treated, remember this: disclose everything except your bottom line. While "You get in enough trouble being honest" is a great moral north star, one can suffer from being—if not too honest—then at least too forthcoming. Sharing too much information with your agent can be expensive. If you were to let even Gandhi know your absolute bottom line when signing his listing agreement, you would likely receive a spate of offers within a horseshoe-toss of that number, possibly depriving you of a higher price.

Trust your fellow man, but recognize the frailty of human nature.

Size Matters

IN THE OPENING SCENE of *Rosencrantz and Guildenstern are Dead,* Rosencrantz correctly calls heads 92 times in a row in a coin-tossing game. While such luck is theoretically possible, Stoppard's play is considered absurdist for an excellent reason. Making money 92 times in a row in real estate is also theoretically possible, but, if anything, is even less likely—about the same as winning the lottery without buying a ticket.

This is why size matters.

Follow these numbers: decades ago—in year one of my real estate career—I bought a duplex in my tumbleweed hometown for $24,000 and made money. A year later, I purchased a four-plex for $60,000 and made money again. The next year we bought a four-plex in San Francisco for $350,000 and did well. The following year, we acquired a couple of industrial buildings for $1.2 million and broke even. (Everyone in the business counts breaking even as making money). Two years later, we developed a shopping center at a cost of $9 million and it turned out well. And finally—the next year—we bought a troubled shopping center for $15.5 million.

In seven years then—over the course of just six purchases—our deal size increased 64,000 percent. Had we continued on that heady trajectory for another seven years, we would have been doing $10 billion projects and been the richest developers on the planet.

It didn't turn out that way.

The day we closed on the troubled center was its finest hour. We had purchased it with shockingly easy money, borrowing 102 percent of the price (we pulled out fees) from our savings and loan partner. Because this benighted center was proof that there is no location so perfect it cannot be ruined through bad design, our grand plan was to raze 80 percent of its cornfield maze of buildings. In the end, however, we could do no more than throw a Band-Aid on the project's terminal defects. Failing in its redevelopment, we rode that property all the way down—imagine Slim Pickens atop the nuclear warhead in *Dr. Strangelove*—until we lost it. It took us some years to recover from the loss.

The episode was rich in lessons (avoiding sociopathic partners among them), but the one to focus on here was the deal's leviathan size relative to our portfolio. If it's axiomatic that sooner or later you will lose money in real estate—it is—then our 64,000 percent increase in deal size was the equivalent of sitting down at a Vegas blackjack table and letting our winnings ride hand after hand after hand.

If you're going to lose money only 10 percent of the time—an optimistic assumption—then if your tenth deal is about the same size as the preceding nine, you will be scorched but not incinerated when it blows. Let's say your niche is $1 million apartment houses that you fix up and sell for $1.3 million and that you manage to stick with that formula. Do it successfully nine times in a row and you've banked $2.7 million. Then when you lose your tenth deal to the bank, your pride will be bruised more than your balance sheet. If, on the other hand, your tenth deal is 64,000 percent larger than your first, its loss could prove a keeper hole on class V rapids. That is, it could force you under water and never let you up.

Take this advice too literally, however, and the world is nothing but duplexes. Grow your deal size, but do it in moderation and manage your risk. By the way, big-picture risk management for developers only comes in a couple of basic colors: the classic tactic is to use other people's money, take fees up front, and never sign recourse, while the long-term investor approach is to avoid spec projects and invest enough equity to weather any storm.

Paraphrasing Goldilocks, just as deals can be too large, they can be too small. If you're humming along doing $1 million apartment houses and someone offers you a $100,000 duplex to rebuild, *don't* do it. Even if it's a guaranteed layup. Why? Because with comparatively so little money involved, you will neither take it seriously nor pay enough attention. You will fail to sit on your architect and thus miss the extravagance of his design. Your contractor's change orders will be so much smaller than those on your bigger projects that they will pile up unchallenged. And you won't be calling your leasing agent every day to find out why the vacancy persists. In the end, you will bounce the ball off the rim.

The trick then is to fight in your weight class. Find deals that fully engage you while, at the same time, allowing you to fight another day if they go bad.

In business at least, size matters.

Buying It Right

IN *ANNA KARENINA*, TOLSTOY BEGINS: "All happy families are alike; each unhappy family is unhappy in its own way." This is true of real estate as well: all happy deals are alike—they start with a motivated seller. Young developers often make the mistake of chasing unlisted properties, listening to brokers who are certain that, if the developer will only offer exactly the right price and terms, the reluctant property owner may consider a sale. You need a couple of these snipe hunts under your belt to learn that it's easier making money flipping burgers than chasing complacent owners. An excellent question to ask whenever someone pitches you a deal is simply: "Why is she selling?" If the answer doesn't involve a compelling need to sell (e.g., death, divorce, dissolution, or disaster), thank the broker for his call and go back to the sports page. The worst answer to this question is: "If she can get her price, the seller will consider it as long as she can find a trade property." This means she will sell only if you pay her an astronomical price and she gets to steal her trade property. Let it go.

Even motivated sellers can—until their time runs out—be unrealistic about their pricing expectations. If you know a seller must sell because of say, estate taxes due, but he's demanding $10 million for a great property worth $7 million, you have a dilemma: do you tie the property up at his price and then gently attempt to educate him about the property's true value (in slightly more pejorative terms, *renegotiate* your deal) or let a competitor charge that particular hill, await his demise, and come in as the second or even the third buyer once the seller has accepted reality? Both strategies entail risk: if you go in first, you're likely to be the first messenger shot, but if you let someone else go first, he just may succeed with his bait-and-switch strategy.

When confronted with an unrealistic seller, we usually advise his broker that teaching market values to a seller is not our business and that we will wait until he learns this from someone else. Thus, we occasionally lose deals.

Far worse, though, is to *win* an overpriced deal. If you chase that $7 million deal for which the seller will only take $10 million and you fall in love with the property or become too invested in closing the deal—you obtain equity commitments from which it would be embarrassing to walk away—and the seller hangs tough and you talk yourself into meeting him half way and paying $8.5 million, you will spend the next three years of your life working for the seller. You handed him your future profits on day one.

If there isn't a country and western song that sobs, "Don't fall in love with nothin' that can't fall in love with you," there should be. If you're looking for love, at least fall for the numbers and not the property. One astute friend ties up properties sight unseen, not even visiting a property until he is in contract at a price he loves. He doesn't want a building's ocean views or historic charm to soften his yield requirements.

The best time to find a motivated and realistic seller is when no one else is buying. "Buy when there's blood in the streets" is the timeless adage. Had you done so in 2009, you would have made a fortune. Market timing is, however, a rare talent, and buying into disaster requires not only a cast-iron stomach and a prophet's certainty of the future, but also the ability to raise patient money when few others can. It might be easier to buy and sell on an established pattern, say, two to three deals a year and then stick with it like a farmer with his annual plantings. By way of example, we have averaged about two new deals a year over the past 35 years, some years not buying anything, others as many as four properties. Schedules and goals aside, it's critical to have the discipline to sit it out when prices make no sense to you.

The best deals sometimes come with the worst contracts. Loan servicers who have foreclosed on choice properties often employ the most obnoxious lawyers, who delight in preparing wickedly one-sided agreements. My advice? If the price, contingencies, and closing date are right, don't worry about the 50 pages of crap in the contract. Agree to buy the property as is, to indemnify the seller, to whatever ridiculous terms the seller insists on, but—as a counterweight—be exceptionally careful with your own due diligence. In particular, insist on a written agreement—an estoppel letter—signed by each tenant of the property that confirms all of the terms of the tenant's lease and the fact that neither tenant nor landlord is in default. And never let a seller convince you to accept his estoppel in lieu of estoppels from the tenants. Why? Because if the seller's substitute estoppel is wrong, and the tenant happens to have a valid offset against rent or the right to terminate or the right to extend the lease for free, all you have is an expensive lawsuit against a seller who already has your money.

As an aside, if there's any way a seller will meet you, do it; become his new best friend. Even if he's tighter than a clam, you will learn something merely by visiting him at his office. And if your closing is subject to anything remotely out of your control—entitlements or new leasing—then the more contact you have with the seller, the more you keep him honestly apprised of what's going on, the better your chances will be of getting the closing date extensions you need to make the deal happen.

Finally, even if you're going to lose $50,000 in due diligence costs, walk away from deals that turn out to be worm-holed. This is easy advice to give and hard to follow, but to succeed, you have to learn when to leave your ante on the table.

Desperately Chasing Yield

TO PARAPHRASE A VULGAR APHORISM, self-delusions are like opinions—
everybody has one. Some have many. Self-delusions are sometimes tragic—
consider starving anorexics who consider themselves fat. Occasionally
self-delusions are merely sad—picture badly aging athletes certain they are
good for another season. And some self-delusions are highly entertaining.
Despite being a perennial finalist for "America's Worst Cook," my dear mother
actually prided herself on her culinary skills.

Self-delusions in real estate are about as rare as fixed professional
wrestling matches. It may be that only pandemic self-delusion can explain
today's pricing of top-quality real estate. It also may be that the usual
suspect—greed—is a major factor.

As of summer 2016, prime office buildings in the country's most desirable
cities (those with ocean views) are at an all-time high, more than 10 percent
greater than their prior peak.

This pricing is not limited to high rises. Any well-located asset considered
bulletproof as to vacancy and rental decline is on fire. First-class regional
shopping malls are fetching the same stratospheric prices as freestanding

McDonald's restaurants (given America's eating habits, these may actually be the safer bet).

Properties deemed "core" by investors hardly need a broker to command a record price. As used in real estate, the term "core" has become so imprecise as to be almost without meaning. Sometimes it signifies that the building so dubbed is within one of the uppermost cities for investing (NYC, SF, LA, DC, Boston, and forget the rest). Sometimes it signifies that the building is in any given city's best neighborhood. Occasionally, it refers to the economic strength of the building's tenants. And it can also merely mean that the building in question matches the rest of the investor's portfolio (another junkyard to an owner of junkyards would be a core asset). Brokers use it as shorthand to message interested buyers, "I guarantee this is a triple-A, no-risk, you're-never-going-to-lose deal."

And therein lie both the sales pitch (a lot of self-delusions are midwived by brokers and consultants) and the rub.

The sales pitch is simple: "Mr. Clever Investor, because you're getting 0.0001 percent on your money in the bank and only 1.82 percent with U.S. Treasury bonds, you really should buy this trophy for a 4 percent return. This core asset is as safe as Treasuries, plus it's a brilliant inflation hedge."

It may be true that you can't cheat an honest man, but cheating a greedy one is a piece of cake, and no one swings at this pitch unless he's desperately chasing yield.

The clever investor might, however, object to the pricing by pointing out that even the best real estate—say a midtown Manhattan trophy building that Donald Trump had nothing to do with—historically sells for less than corporate Baa bonds. And that today, that bond rate is 4.79 percent. The indefatigable broker will concede the poor initial return but swear the overall return on investment (the internal rate of return or "IRR") will be splendid if one holds the building ten years and sells it then for a whopping profit. (For more on the IRR, see the Glossary and chapter 16).

This is where the self-delusions come in, however induced. Anyone with enough money to buy real estate must know that interest rates are bound to rise. So a buyer has to convince herself she can somehow outrace the avalanche of falling prices that will rumble right behind rising interest rates.

On the plus side, there are a lot of fun choices: "We'll get out of this deal before rates run up." Or, "Even though the building is fully leased, we, with our special expertise, will painlessly double rents as the leases turn over." Or, "We're buying this for the next generation." Or, back to the IRR—the calculation that sank a thousand ships—"Our fully leveraged IRR yield will be at least 8.5 percent no matter what happens to rates."

Far better—or at least much cheaper—to be self-deluded about one's youthful looks or charm or killer jump shot.

Liquid Assets

I ALWAYS WANTED TO MAKE THE FRONT PAGE of the *Wall Street Journal*...
until I did. The December 12, 2014, *WSJ* showed our Healdsburg, California,
shopping center doing an excellent imitation of McCovey Cove during a
Giants game, replete with canoers and kayakers. This picturesque scene,
of course, made the happy-talk news on local television. I wish I could say
we were delighted to add a bit of levity to the storm that battered northern
California.

Lake McNellis was short-lived, and its damage was relatively minor. We
were quite fortunate, for parking lots can readily fail beneath oceanic weight,
landscaping can be washed away, shops ruined, inventory destroyed, and the
drying process long and expensive.

Even in drought-wracked California, rivers flood. And when a town is
built on a riverbank, as Healdsburg is on the Russian River, all of the storm
drains, culverts, and flood prevention measures one can muster are merely a
lesson in futility—if not humility—when the almost perfect storm rolls in.

We cannot prevent floods or earthquakes or fires, riots, terrorists, or even little greasy kitchen fires that inevitably cause either more damage than one has insurance for or not enough to cover the deductible.

In times of breathtaking prices for real estate, it may be appropriate to put the flood question more broadly and ask if any building is truly as safe as so many buyers would love to believe.

Yes, it's possible to own a building or two for even a very long time without suffering casualty losses. But a whole portfolio over an extended career? That's not statistically possible. Yet, if an owner is truly prudent in buying insurance, it will cover most of her direct losses arising from an accident. Indirect losses are another matter, however, and often as not go uncompensated. As it happened, we had flood insurance for Healdsburg, but because we also had a five-figure deductible, we definitely paid for the pleasure of helping the *WSJ* sell newspapers.

Let's leave the world of cinematic losses that seldom occur and consider a more common way to watch values vanish: no-holds-barred competition. We might call this "Houston roulette" because Houston's laissez-faire approach to zoning is one of Texas's lasting charms. Subject to a building permit alone, developers are free to build anything they like, anywhere they like, anytime they want. But live by the dollar, die by it. Cities with minimal regulations and barriers for developers often end up in situations in which no project is safe from competition. If you build a 75-story high rise and advertise the finest views, your ex-partner can build 100 stories out of spite tomorrow and tout even better views. You build a supermarket at the best intersection in town and overnight your competitor assembles three parcels across the street and throws up an even snazzier market. One of you dies.

Where land is plentiful and approvals are easy to obtain, economic obsolescence—and breathtaking loss—requires no more than an idiot with a pot of money and a dream of a new building next to yours. The formula of doom is as simple as the Pythagorean theorem: developer + money + easy zoning = death-spiral overbuilding.

This is exactly why smart money loves core properties. Because developers can somehow always come up with the money (let's face it, that's what they do), the best defense is to own properties in the handful of coastal cities in which the zoning and approval process is akin to medieval torture.

Yet even a building as safe as kindergarten loses value every year through what too many view as merely a tax benefit—depreciation. Rather than simply a happy paper loss on April 15, depreciation is real—buildings eventually wear out. The Internal Revenue Service (IRS) has decreed that 39 and a half years is the standard useful life for buildings, and it allows a 2.5 percent deduction for depreciation every year. This also means—because the IRS has it about right—that your building is cooked when your depreciation burns off. Your children can either scrape your worn-out building and start fresh or go the more expensive route of gutting and rebuilding it.

Either way, all you have left is your residual land value. If you have chosen your land carefully—on high ground yet within walking distance of big water (maybe a little farther than our shopping center)—your land appreciation should more than offset your building loss. If not, you might be reminded of the old joke: How do you make a small fortune in real estate? Start with a large one.

A Little Help from My Friends

LIGHTHOUSE KEEPERS CAN DO IT BY THEMSELVES. Developers can't.

That said, new developers typically need to pull off at least their first deal on their own, playing every instrument in the orchestra: investment broker, leasing and mortgage broker, contractor, day laborer, property manager, janitor, lawyer, and even accountant. There is a benefit to this wearying exertion: just as a conductor knows how all of his musicians should sound, you should have a good feel for what your service providers do, and trying it yourself is a quick way to get it.

As a developer, you can stay small—doing fixer-uppers—and be a one-man band. That option would be a mistake for the ambitious. The moment you can afford to have someone else do it, your time will be too valuable to waste painting houses, chasing loan quotes, or keeping books. If you have the desire to tackle larger, more complicated projects, you will need help, particularly with the skills you lack. The question is, should your help come from consultants, employees, or partners?

First, let's put money back in the drawer. Financial partners are far too important to be lumped with any others in the development process. They—and their pros and cons—will be dealt with separately in an ensuing chapter.

If prudence means more to you than an old-fashioned name, your ascent from solo act to major development firm should entail an interim step of employing consultants and service providers on an hourly basis only. As long as you can rent any profession—legal, architectural, engineering, whatever—*and* still get the service you need (that is, first-rate work on the day you need it), you will be far better off renting rather than buying. Initially, the math is simple: if you are spending $100,000 a year in legal fees and your lawyer is making $200,000 at her firm, it would be crazy to hire her. (Yet rookies sometimes do, trying to impress the outside world with their size). Less intuitively, even if your outside legal bills were to increase to $300,000 a year and you could hire her for $200,000, the flexibility you retain—you can cap a consultant like a rotten pipe—may well be worth the extra $100,000. Employees are expensive. No one ever lays off a suddenly superfluous employee on the first day a big project is lost; months drag on before even the flintiest developer pulls the trigger.

Renting rather than buying help is obvious. As obvious, but as often ignored, is the way to get the best service from your consultants. First and foremost: pay your bills on receipt. Second: treat your consultants with friendship, kindness, and respect. Make them feel part of your team. Lunches, drinks, and handwritten thank-you notes work wonders with harried service providers. On the flip side, if you question his bill, if you tell your consultant he should have finished his task in ten hours rather than the 20 he billed, you're accusing him of, at best, incompetence. He will understandably take this criticism as an affront to his integrity. Rather than continue to employ—and badger—a resentful consultant who's going to bottom-pile your work, negotiate his bill if you must, pay him, and replace him. Don't commute over burned bridges.

The trick to getting the highest quality work from consultants is this: hire the most experienced person you can afford who will actually do your work.

Remember, you are always hiring an individual, not her company or firm. It does you no good to hire the fanciest firm in town if a junior associate who knows less about real estate than your mother-in-law is assigned your work. One way to adopt this precept is to hire well-seasoned sole practitioners.

Last point on consultants: think Noah's ark. You need two of each of them—two contractors, two architects, two engineers, two escrow officers, and so on. And they should know about one another. Why? Because, putting aside competition's salutary effects on service and cost, you need a backup plan. Life trumps business and, sooner or later, your favorite consultant will be unavailable to you, perhaps at your deal's most critical moment.

You can outsource your entire orchestra for a good while, but one sunny day you will be sitting in a fancy office, working a deal, when the bemused seller will interrupt your pitch to ask, "Who's this *we*?" If a single pilot can't land the plane, and you achieved *we* only by throwing in your border collie, it's time to bring in either partners or key employees.

This can be a tough choice.

While employees will cost you more than partners if you fail or have only middling success, they are cheap if you are truly successful. If you knock the ball out of the park and believe you could have done so without them, your partners will prove inordinately expensive. And the extra cost of partners may be misspent. Doling out a partnership interest doesn't automatically buy you better or more loyal help. Employees are often as dedicated and capable as partners. But, properly viewed, life's about the journey and not what's left in your suitcase at your last stop. The trip is easier—and more enjoyable—with others helping to shoulder your losses and share in your victories. While we have all been through bad or ill-suited partners—you may have to kiss a few frogs to find your business soul mate—many of my successful friends have had career-long partners. Without mine—Beth Walter and Mike Powers have been partners with me since the early '80s—I would have ended up managing a hotel on the Mosquito Coast.

It's your call.

Fickle Shades of Green

"Friendship is constant in all other things save in the office and affairs of love."

SHAKESPEARE HAD IT RIGHT. And money is less constant than love. Even if your project is profitable, the money that loved you when you first put together your deal can grow distant, even hostile, over the course of the investment. And if things do go wrong, the principal advantage a partnership has over a marriage—ironclad dissolution rights—can cause a developer a world of grief. In short, a dollar-denominated relationship is one of those wrong places to go looking for love.

Instead of love, seek understanding; seek money that listens. While capital is seldom a great listener—money talks—one type of capital available to real estate is distinctly harder of hearing than the other.

Almost everyone starts with family and friends' money (F&F). Also known as country club money, this is your preferred form of outside equity. You will get the best economic deal from your friends, you will have more control over your project, and, typically, you will be more difficult to dethrone should your deal sputter.

The F&F profit-sharing formula hasn't changed since the dawn of capitalism: from the project's cash flow, the equity gets a preferred return a few percent higher than Treasury bills (say about 5 percent) and, once that's paid, any remaining cash is split 50/50 between money and developer. If the project entails less work, risk, or return than a ground-up development—such as a simple lease-up on an empty building—then the split might be 80 to the equity, 20 to the developer. When the project is sold or refinanced, the proceeds are first used to bring the preferred return current and then to repay the equity in full. And then any remaining proceeds are divided 50/50 (or 80/20 in the simpler deals).

Assuming you want outside partners (whether you should is a later chapter), F&F is the way for you to start and what you should stick with as long as you can. F&F investors are, by definition, your friends and they—in the beginning at least—will listen to your explanations about why you missed your performance benchmarks. They may even be mildly sympathetic. And because they neither will be real estate professionals nor have the rights in your partnership agreement that professionals would insist on, they will likely have little choice but to ride out the bad times with you. Even if the love is gone. (If you want to go to heaven, never accept money from anyone unless you are certain he can readily afford the loss of his investment; far too many guys will raid their kids' college funds for a risky venture just to act like hitters.)

The chief drawback of F&F money is obvious: unless you picked your parents and college roommates on the basis of their balance sheets, this is at best a quarter tank of gas. When you empty-pocket the last of your friends, you will be running on fumes about the time you need to fund your next big deal.

In contrast, the other equity's proven reserves are beyond measurement. Institutional money flows from multiple headwaters and—as long as you don't need it—is always readily available. It costs more than F&F money and is basically deaf. Called *hot money* for good reason, it will burn a serious hole in your deal—if not you—if you fail to deliver on time. How? Through the unholy miracle of compound interest. Rather than the simple interest of, say, 5 percent asked by F&F investors, institutional money demands a compounded annual return as high as 15 to 20 percent before you share in any profits. Using an IRR approach, this formula adds the cash flow the equity receives each year to its share of sales proceeds and then calculates the rate of interest on the total thus paid. If that return fails to exceed the equity's minimum required yield, you receive nothing. This, by the way, is a common result for developers in institutional joint ventures. If you can build, lease, and sell your project on budget and on time, you should do well with institutional money. But a delay or a significant cost overrun may mean that your partner gets a 14 percent return instead of the 15 percent it required and you get an expensive life lesson.

And if things do go poorly with your project and you start begging for relief, your institutional partner's attitude may remind you of Tommy Lee Jones in *The Fugitive*. Moments before he leaps into the abyss from atop an enormous dam, a desperate Harrison Ford swears, "I'm innocent." Ready to gun him down, U.S. Marshall Tommy Lee replies, "I don't care."

Instead of love, look for money that listens. You want the best economic deal you can get from your money partner, but you also want someone with patience and understanding, someone who is content to be your partner even when the fan gets clogged.

Autographing the Deal

12

IT SEEMS WE ALL LIE. Depending on which lying study you choose to believe, we tell somewhere between a couple and a couple hundred lies a day. The lower number is found among monks who have taken a vow of silence while the higher number counts days attending conventions. Most of our lies are harmless enough, pumping ourselves up, making others feel better, beveling society's hard edges.

But if believed, one persistent lie—"I never sign personal guaranties"— can traumatize a young developer. If she overhears a corrida of aging bulls swearing they haven't signed a guaranty since 1999 and then complains to her banker of how unfairly she's being treated, it will likely be unpleasant. And if she decides to shop bankers, she will be wasting everyone's time.

Oversimplifying matters slightly, two basic loans predominate in real estate: lower-risk permanent loans for stabilized assets (a ten-year loan on a fully leased office building) and higher-risk construction loans (an 18-month loan to build an apartment house). Although nonrecourse debt, permanent loans universally contain "carve-out" guaranties in which the borrower promises he will properly maintain the property and use the rent from the property to pay the mortgage, taxes, expenses, and so on. If he intentionally wrongs the property or the lender—if he takes the rent to Vegas—he will be personally liable. Commonly known as the *bad boy* provisions, these are signed by everybody.

And everyone signs guaranties whenever they're doing construction. Everyone is signing autographs. The rich and sometimes the clever can avoid *repayment* guaranties—a guaranty that the construction loan itself will be repaid—but everyone inks a *completion* guaranty—a promise that all construction will be finished and paid for. Guaranteeing completion rather than repayment is lights-out better for a borrower. Why? Because as long as you finish the building, you can toss the keys on your lender's desk if your anchor tenant goes bankrupt before your grand-opening party or you find yourself unable to repay the loan for any other sad reason (there are more than a few).

The bull may tell you he doesn't sign bad-boy or completion guaranties either, but if you press him, he will admit some well-capitalized entity he owns or controls signs for him. The lender still gets the ink. And even when bank underwriting standards are melting like crayons on a desert dashboard, you will be guaranteeing everything but the outcome of the Super Bowl if you're trying to finance your first couple of development deals.

It's impossible to argue with the advice you hear at every industry cocktail party—"Never guarantee nothing." Yet guaranties staring one in the face can have a salutary effect. Like rock-climbing Yosemite's Half Dome, it has a way of focusing one's attention. If it is *your* personal net worth on the line, you will truly vet the deal, tweak the risks, and verify that approvals are in hand, construction costs fully quantified, the tenants as creditworthy as advertised, and so on. In short, knowing it's your guaranty may make you climb down from a deal you shouldn't have attempted in the first place. If not sharing in a project's potentially fatal abyss makes you a little less careful—it does—and you do a regrettable deal, you may not be personally liable for the loan, but your partners will have lost their investment and you will have nothing to show for a couple of years' worth of effort but a slammed reputation.

"Hear you, dude, but can you skip the pontificating and tell me instead how I get around guaranties?"

You do what the bulls do. You get the bank to waive it by putting up more equity and accepting a higher interest rate on the loan. Or, if you want to keep your equity down, you skip the banks and go straight to the debt funds (Blackstone, Starwood, etc.) and pay a lot more interest. There's a problem, however, with this approach for a young developer: a rich guy may not care too much if his lender demands more equity because his idle cash is earning 0.015 percent interest (also known as *nothing*) in the bank. On the other hand, you should really care because rather than malingering in six-month certificates of deposit, your idle cash is jingling in your pocket. You are using Other People's Money (OPM) for your equity, all of which carries a much higher coupon rate than bank debt. The banks are in the 2 to 4 percent range; OPM costs anywhere from 5 to 12 percent—meaning that every dollar of OPM kicks your dented can of profit a little farther down the road. (OPM could also be an abbreviation for "Others Profit instead of Me.")

But you counter with the old saw that you would rather sleep well than eat well. Not bad as bromides go, but there's a word for a developer with no money or risk in the deal: *consultant*. If you're not taking any risk, you're going to be starving. Your financial partners may not be theoretical physicists, but they usually have an intuitive feel for business. They know that if you are putting up nothing more than your time and your rapidly expiring purchase contract, they can hire you rather than partner with you.

Take this home: there is no way to make real developer profits without taking at least some real developer risks. No risk, no reward. That said, you should try your best to limit risks: have tenants do their own improvements in exchange for a fixed contribution, outsource everything (nothing runs up a tab like employees), and never hire your college roommate as your general contractor. (Having your contractor go belly-up during construction is one of the rockier roads to ruin.)

And, of course, listen to the old guys: guarantee as little as possible. Or better yet, choose your deals with infinite caution and then, like diving off the ten-meter board, your guaranty will only look scary.

13

The Politics of It All

Rents and occupancy rates are tumbling today in North Dakota because shale oil is mud in a $35-a-barrel world. Once it was the hottest real estate market in America; now a northerly is blowing across the prairies and landlords are scarcely better insulated than shale's jobless roughnecks. This turnabout is not unique to the Dakotas. Properly viewed, the lords of real estate are always bit players, mere vendors to the stars who make economies twinkle. As long as a gold rush rampages, we do well renting tents and cabins. But, sooner or later, mines peter out.

If real estate is no more resilient than its surrounding economy—it isn't—and if all economies eventually falter—they do—how does a prudent investor protect herself, particularly if she is buying into a bull market's heat?

The best way to protect yourself from the next correction requires a skill few possess; namely, the ability to call your shot, to time the market perfectly, and to sell at its peak. If you happen to have this rare talent, forget real estate and go straight to Wall Street. (By the way, a *correction* occurs when others get creamed, a *crash* when you do.)

For less farsighted mortals, buying with all equity—using little or no debt—is a fair if timid strategy. It works well enough for the rich, but it is a poor option for someone starting out. If you can convince your investors to put up 100 percent of a purchase price, leaving you risk free, they will convince you to give them 100 percent of the profits, leaving you profit free.

The second-best way to protect yourself against loss is to create so much value that you will still be afloat when the tide bottoms out. Combined with a conservative level of debt (say 50 to 60 percent), this is also the best way to make a lasting fortune. While it is sometimes true that value can be created through a brilliant purchase, stealing property—despite what you may hear at conferences—is hard. By and large, sellers tend to be smart enough and, when they are dumb, their stupidity more often lies in mulishly overvaluing their holdings than in wanting to give them away.

Doing something—anything—to a property can create value. But the easier the makeover, or the more obvious it is, the less value you will create. If you buy an empty building, paint it, re-landscape it, and lease it out, you may have created lasting value or you may have simply caught the leasing market's next wave. Unless the building's vacancy was truly a result of inept ownership (as your broker will swear) rather than of market conditions, your paint and petunias may have left the property's shortcomings unresolved. Consider selling it.

If, instead, you demolish that building and build a new project in its place—or build fresh on an empty lot—you will have created lasting value, but the question will be for whom. If the property was already zoned to permit your new project or if it's in a town where rezoning is easier than skateboarding, then chances are your dumb seller baked most of your eventual profit into his asking price. And, if you pay his price, you could end up spending a couple of years of your life having effectively worked for him, leaving you with a shiny new project worth about what it cost to build.

Once in a great while you can do something to a property that no one else has thought of and hit it big. The first guy to tie up a major luxury apartment complex at apartment prices, convert it into condominiums, and then sell it off at condo prices made enough to retire the national debt. The second guy not so much. Why? Because it took the dumb sellers five seconds to add the downstream condo profit to the pricing of every other apartment building on the market once the play was public.

And that leads us to an excellent way of either creating lasting value or, if you don't get the votes, losing the sitting part of your anatomy: rezoning property in first-class towns, where it's a lot harder than skateboarding. Smart guys—particularly smart guys who have enough money—will tell you to never buy unzoned property. They will insist that you close only after you have your final city approvals. This great advice is comparatively easy to follow in down markets or fly-over cities, but if you're going to develop in the best locations, sooner or later you will be buying—or handing over so much option money you might as well be buying—unzoned property. And praying for votes at city hall.

We have arrived—at last—at politics. The next chapter will give you a few hard-learned lessons in the art of rezoning in recalcitrant cities. But before getting to those, it may be worth leaving you with something to ponder, namely, the politicians' view of their relationship with developers. The legendary Jesse Unruh, czar of California's Assembly in the 1960s, nailed it when he opined, "If you can't eat their food, drink their booze, take their money, and then vote against them, you've got no business being up here."

Decked by City Hall?

JESSE UNRUH'S ADMONISHMENT IS WELL WORTH REMEMBERING by anyone seeking property entitlements. You may march into city hall thinking you have the votes, judging from your conversations with council members, but their private promises can fade the moment the public hearing turns contentious. It's not that politicians are necessarily duplicitous, it's that they consider themselves protectors of the public good while deeming you—no matter your honesty—hopelessly self-interested. Owning this lofty moral high ground, politicians can justify behavior toward developers that would raise eyebrows in Hell.

And, let's face it, the angry neighbors are often right: your city doesn't need another traffic-clogging monument to stucco. But even if your project would be the best thing to hit town since fluoridated water, it is still easy to lose. The trick is to help the politicians help you. Give them the ammunition—or more accurately, the cover—they need to vote for you.

Here are a few suggestions:

First, figure out who your opposition is and why they care. Meet with them. Compromise—reduce the project a little or throw in another public benefit—and then meet with them again. Repeat this procedure until you can look the planning director in the eye and tell him you're tapped out. He will, of course, know you're not, but will nevertheless appreciate your efforts.

Second, figure out who runs the town. Cities where you want to develop tend to require three levels of approval—an architectural review committee, a planning commission, and city council. Dominated as they are by prima donna design professionals, architectural review committees are sometimes wildly annoying, but they seldom have real power. It does happen on occasion, however, that the second tier—the planning commission—is the true decision maker with a timid council reluctant to overrule it on appeal. More often, the city council controls major projects, and it is there your ultimate efforts must be directed. There are, however, cities where the mayor or even the city manager has inordinate influence over the process and must be individually persuaded of your project's civic value.

Meet with the decision makers at the outset but advise them that you are going to honor the approval process, that before you even file your application, you will meet with the neighborhood and the planning department to solicit suggestions and opinions. And do exactly that. Only then, after your first several meetings, do you formally file your development application.

If you are young, personable, and not obviously wealthy, handle your city meetings yourself. If you are not, hire an entitlements professional to represent you. Definitely have someone else represent you if you see nothing amiss in the following anecdote: while campaigning in West Virginia, a wealthy politician once grandly proclaimed to a bar jam-packed with miners, "A beer for the house and a Courvoisier for me."

Try to meet individually with each of the board members—architectural, planning, and city council—before their public hearings. This is time consuming and sometimes painful, but it is the only way for any challenging project to be fully understood. If any representatives refuse to meet with you—they often do—then write them a letter outlining why your project should be approved. And remember that as part of the public record your letter will be subject to scrutiny by your opposition. Keep it short, straight-forward, and factual.

Have a neighborhood outreach meeting before every public hearing, put your project in its best light, and hope like hell you can garner a few supporters. Getting a controversial project approved requires at least some disinterested public support—that is, backing from individuals who will gain nothing from its construction. The city council will discount—if not dismiss—support from the construction unions, your next-door neighbor whose property value will double, and the nonprofits you will enrich as part of your project's public benefits. You need genuine support. Fortunately, even the greenest council member knows support is much harder to muster than opposition. This is why a handful of independent supporters can offset a room full of opponents. And if you do manage to recruit well-intentioned neighbors to speak on your behalf, remember them afterwards with a handwritten thank-you note or, better yet, chocolates or flowers. (What would you want in return for spending a whole evening at a public hearing on behalf of a stranger?)

Leave your Rolex, Porsche, and, whenever possible, your lawyer at home when attending project meetings. Bringing a lawyer is a lot like hissing "Don't you know who I am?" to a hostess when she tells you there's a 45-minute wait for a table. It shows you've already lost.

Never take a cell phone call—or check e-mail or game scores—during any meeting, no matter how mind-numbingly protracted it becomes. There may come a point during the council meeting when the city clerk announces the next five neighborhood speakers in advance. And, since you've already had ten public meetings, you know that each of them would rather see you crucified than your project approved. Even so, you must sit there and politely listen to their concerns. When you can no longer follow this last rule, it's time to hang up your spurs. (I had to.)

Finally, tell the truth and keep your word. You might as well admit your project's drawbacks or civic costs because if it's controversial enough, it will all come out anyway. And everyone remembers the promises you make in a public hearing. Keep them.

Sell versus Hold

SOME DECISIONS IN LIFE ARE EASIER THAN OTHERS. Deciding whether you want fries with that is a piece of cake. Deciding to tell a remorseful friend the truth about his new tattoo is considerably harder. Among the hardest decisions in real estate is determining whether to keep or sell a finished project. Do you sell the disco while they're still dancing or does it become a transgenerational asset?

To answer this question, a newly minted developer might consider taking a deep breath and first asking herself where she wants to be in 20 years. Does she want to be a media darling running a big company and doing the splashiest deals in town, or would she prefer to work on building her cash flow and net worth? While not by definition mutually exclusive, these two objectives often work out that way. You're better off deciding the big picture question *before* you do your first deal because without a goal and a strategy to reach it, you may find yourself not only making poor tactical decisions, but also unable to make the right ones. In other words, unless you plan in advance, the sell/hold decision may prove a luxury you cannot afford.

Oversimplifying the menu, development firms come in two basic flavors: merchant and investment builders—that is, those who sell everything upon completion and those who never sell. And, of course, countless firms hybridize these distinct businesses.

The classic build-to-sell approach, merchant building has two principal advantages over its counterpart: the ability to do many more deals and to profit much sooner. Merchants can do more deals because their required returns on cost are lower than those of investors. They typically charge greater fees for the acquisition and construction of their projects and sell them as soon as they are finished. Merchants are about fees and sale proceeds now; merchants are about ordinary income. (In real estate, *now* is a relative term. Even the swiftest projects take at least two years before you can cash in and more likely a minimum of three to five years from the moment you first see a property to the day you sell.)

The stodgier strategy, investment building is the build-to-hold approach. To keep a property long term, an investment builder needs a going-in return well in excess of the merchant's. He charges his project little in the way of front-end fees. Investors are about cash flow later; investors are about capital gains. Turning an old expression on its head, investors mortgage the present for the sake of the future.

Merchants typically seek an overall return on cost of about 100 basis points—1 percent—greater than the cap rate at which they expect to sell the property. (The term "cap rate" or "capitalization rate" is explained at length in the Glossary). Thus, if he anticipates a cap rate on sale of 6 percent, the merchant will develop for a 7 percent return on total cost. As long as prices remain steady or rise, the merchant will profit handsomely on the sale, but— here's the point—not so handsomely as to enable him to keep his project for the long term. To do so, he would have to leave too much equity, earning too little return, in the deal. In short, he is forced to sell.

For a similar project, investors will require a return on cost 200 basis points—2 percent—greater than the expected sale cap rate, an 8 percent return on cost if cap rates are six. If you wish to be an investment builder, this higher requirement means two things: (1) because you will be competing with merchants with lower return thresholds, you will be less competitive and winning far fewer deals; but (2) you will be able to retain your projects for the long term.

In short, unless your return on a project's total cost is roughly 2 percent higher (or more) than the cap rate at which you can sell the property, you will be economically compelled to sell it. You will have no sell versus hold decision to make.

To bring this point home, it may be worth summarizing our firm's strategy: we're more interested in having fewer, higher-quality properties with lower debt than we are in amassing a portfolio to pay overhead. And we never intentionally develop a property with a merchant approach—that is, one for which the only exit strategy is a sale. Why? Simply put, we think it's too risky. Merchant building works great in good times, but the moment the market slips—and it will—that 100-basis-point spread can disappear overnight. While the investment builder isn't impervious to loss in a down market—everyone loses money sooner or later—he's on far safer ground.

We try to always develop to investor yield standards—that 200-point spread—but we still sell about two-thirds of the projects we develop. Why? In the beginning, we had to, we needed to eat and, because it takes five to seven years to start building meaningful cash flow on a pure investment build approach, one can easily starve as an investor. We continue selling today for the simple reason that many properties are at their best on day one.

When do we choose to sell? We sell if, despite our best efforts, our return on cost comes in too low (either because of construction cost overruns or our failure to achieve anticipated rents). We sell when the barriers-to-entry for our project's future competitors are low or when we have concerns about either our tenants' longevity or the quality of our location. And conversely, we keep our high-yielding properties in competition-constrained environments.

If you want to run a big development firm, become a merchant builder. If you want the luxury of deciding which deals to keep and slowly building your cash flow, consider investment building. But if you go the investor route, choose the properties you keep carefully—many do have their finest hour at the ribbon cutting.

Lies, Damn Lies, and the IRR

OUTRIGHT FRAUD IN SALES PACKAGES is about as rare as total amnesia. However negligently prepared the offerings may be, they seldom contain jaw-dropping lies. If one says a property's current gross income is $1 million, it usually is. And simple offerings—say, a flyer pasted together by a residential broker selling a gas station—are seldom far off track. Why? Purported facts about the present are subject to verification, painful lawsuits spawn in the waters of outright deception, and the shallow-end players are careful.

So, too, are the sophisticates swimming in real estate's deep end, but they can achieve depths smaller fish can only dream of. Through the magic of the IRR, the big sharks can claim to be able to foretell the future. And while facts about the present are subject to door-pounding process servers, gilt-edged projections about the future are not.

An IRR calculation is simple in theory: one takes the projected annual cash flow an investor hopes to receive from a property for a given holding period—usually ten years—and adds to that the property's estimated sale value in the tenth year and then uses the combined sum to calculate the total return on investment (or IRR) over that ten-year period. So, if a property pays

5 percent in annual cash flow over ten years and then sells at the end of that tenth year for twice what the investor originally paid, the IRR would be not quite 11 percent. This plays a lot better in a prospectus than a measly 5 percent return.

It's worth pointing out that if one assumes that rents and expenses remain constant during the ten-year period (this assumption will often prove wildly optimistic) and that the selling cap rate ten years out will be the same as the buying cap rate today (more optimism), the IRR will be identical to the cap rate paid today. In other words, if you bought it at a 6 cap and received a 6 percent yield for the ten years you owned it, then sold it for exactly what you paid for it, your IRR would be 6 percent, the same as your initial cap rate.

The breathtaking fallacy behind every IRR analysis ever prepared is obvious: it assumes that one can predict highly complex and interrelated financial conditions—interest rates, capitalization rates, tenant demand, new competition, population growth, personal income shifts, and so on—ten years hence. A mere handful of people predicted the crash of 2008–2009, and they did so only a year or two in advance. In 2009, absolutely no one predicted that apartment prices would be soaring in 2011 or that A-quality commercial-building prices would equal their all-time highs.

Predicting how real estate will price in ten years is, simply put, impossible. It's akin to accurately predicting rainfall totals in 2026.

But knowing that they'd have as much luck picking the 2026 Super Bowl winner as in nailing long-range prices deters almost no one in real estate's upper echelons. Glossy high-end sales brochures and investment committee reports routinely contain impressive-looking Argus spreadsheets that magically produce the IRR the buyer or investment committee desires. The magic is easier than voodoo—you just keep raising the anticipated tenth-year sales price until the desired IRR is hit. Who is going to be around in ten years to tell the analyst she was wrong? Commissions and careers will be made and remade and bonuses paid many times over before the truth will out.

A buyer would have more fun—and get just as reliable information—consulting a fortune-teller.

Alternative interpretations of the IRR acronym such as "inflated rate of return" or "I rationalize risk" should come to the mind of anyone confronted with reams of spreadsheets predicting rising rents, falling expenses, zero vacancy factors, and impressively low cap rates.

That the old-school return on investment, or ROI, calculation is a much more precise measurement of financial performance means it's of no value to large swaths of the real estate community. Its accuracy renders it too dismal a tool to be helpful to anyone selling the sizzle. A proper ROI calculation ignores cap rates and interest rates (by assuming a property is held free and clear, it deprives one of the funhouse-mirror distortions created by leverage) and looks only at what a property's net operating income will be upon construction completion and full lease-up. If one has a fair bit of preleasing and a construction contract in hand when solving for ROI, this calculation can be quite accurate. For those selling the future as a far rosier place than today, this is devastating.

We all have our self-delusions. However, having them about numbers and the future values of our acquisitions can be an expensive mistake.

Working without a Net Worth

CASH FLOW IS REAL ESTATE'S REAL VALUE.

Franklin D. Roosevelt's first vice president, John Nance "Cactus Jack" Garner, is remembered for having observed that the vice presidency wasn't worth a bucket of warm spit. Except he didn't say spit. The difference between the vice presidency and a financial statement is that the latter is occasionally worth a bucket full.

As a young developer, I could never convince my bankers of the grandeur of my financial statements. A standard financial statement was then—as it is today—little more than a compilation of one's net worth. As 99.4 percent of my net worth consisted of the "equity" I held in our various limited partnerships, my bankers were not nearly as impressed as they might have been. Holding my statement at arm's length (as one might a diamondback), my banker would patiently explain that while my 5 percent subordinate-to-everyone general-partnership interest may indeed be worth millions, her principal concern was debt repayment: where would my loan payments come from and what was my cash flow? Because my cash flow at the time was permanently dammed somewhere far upstream, I thought this line of questioning rather impertinent.

But maybe she had a point.

Soberly viewed, a financial statement is more daydream than fact. If someone claims he's worth a wildly crazy amount—say a Silicon Valley fortune of $300 million—that's a lovely reverie, but the chances of that guy actually coming up with $300 million in cash are slim. First, instead of the pipe-dream number he claims on his statement for the illiquid asset that constitutes the vast bulk of his empire, he has to mark that asset down to market, be it stock in a privately held company, timber, a coal mine, whatever. Then, he has to sell it, pay federal and state taxes, and—if he's married—divide that sum by two.

If he owns that $300 million in stock in a publicly traded company, that means he's the chief executive and can't sell because his holdings are in stock options or are contractually or de facto restricted. (The CEO can't be seen dumping his company's stock.)

While financial statements are generally more exaggerated than circus-tent revivals, they are particularly worthless in real estate. Thanks to the miracle of the 1031 tax-deferred exchange, if a real estate entrepreneur has been around long enough to be truly successful, his current properties—say they show $10 million in equity—will likely trace their tax-basis origins back over 30 years and involve a dozen 1031 exchanges. This means his assets will have tremendous negative bases for tax purposes and likely carry a latent tax liability often surpassing the claimed equity. The only way for a real estate mogul to sell without triggering this tax—dying—has yet to be widely embraced.

Putting real estate's idiosyncrasies aside, financial statements are still problematic. Even if a financial statement were to accurately reflect the market value of assets and deduct the inchoate taxes, issues likely linger. How would you prefer your own personal $10 million net worth—assets of $10 million and liabilities of $0, or assets of $3.01 billion and liabilities of $3 billion? An over-leveraged net worth can, back to Cactus Jack, bubble away like spit on a griddle.

And even assuming you chose curtain No. 1—the $10 million free and clear—that doesn't say beans about your cash flow, my nagging banker's original concern. Ten million dollars parked with Wells Fargo may be safe, but it nets you nearly nothing at today's interest rates. Ten million dollars in gold or any growth stock is good for a nice round zero in annual income, while $10 million in Treasury bonds has a pulse somewhere between zero and 3 percent, depending on term. And quality corporate bonds? A tad higher than Treasuries.

So this is where real estate finally pays off, where maybe we're not so dumb after all for having chosen this profession. (When I was quizzing my editor about numbers to illustrate this point, I asked her how much money one needed to be really rich; she countered by asking whether we were talking Silicon Valley rich or just real estate rich. Sighing, I dropped the question.) Anyway, an enviably solid real estate portfolio worth $10 million could easily net $500,000 to $700,000 a year in stable, recurring cash flow, far better than its obvious alternatives. My banker was right—it is all about cash flow.

To paraphrase Mark Twain: When I was a young man of 30, my bankers were so ignorant I could hardly stand to have them around. But when I got to be 40, I was astonished by how much they had learned in ten years.

Monogamy and Its Downside

BANKERS LIKE EXCLUSIVITY, but developers should be less enamored.

A picture of a smiling developer and a happy banker shaking hands could illustrate Wikipedia's explanation of "symbiotic relationship." Developers need to borrow and bankers need to lend, despite their occasional issues with regulators. We could almost end this chapter right there, but a few nuances in this often happy relationship are worth touching on.

Unless the announcement of your birth appeared in the *New York Times*, you have to get started somewhere and, for successful deals at least, a banker's money is always the cheapest in town—far cheaper, no matter the interest rate, than giving away half the deal. Yes, rookie developers must part with nearly everything regardless. But with a bit of luck, they may over time be able to decide for themselves how much to rely on banks versus equity partners.

Veteran developers usually argue in favor of partners, noting that you have to personally guarantee bank debt whereas you promise your equity partners nada (at least in the fine print). However, if you are going to feel a moral obligation—forget the partnership agreement's absolution—to repay your investors, you're better off guaranteeing bank debt; your ethical and legal obligations are identical and you get to keep all the profits. Also, personal guaranties have the side benefit of focusing your attention on the moment at hand—in this case, your deal's underwriting. Sooner or later, we all lose money, but perhaps a bit less often when it is our own money.

So, a banker is a successful developer's best friend. But *the* first time you try to borrow more than a cup of sugar, your banker will want a committed, monogamous relationship. She will want all of your business. She will shake hands and promise she will take care of all your needs; she will lend you every dollar you will ever need. And she will mean it. Your BFF with financial benefits. Here's the problem—you can't shake hands with a corporation.

Despite the best intentions in the world, your banker is only as good as the last loan she committed to you. Although she may truly become a close friend over time, likely as not she will quit, retire, be fishing, or be in the hospital the week you absolutely need a loan commitment. Or, her bank will be merged out of existence (this has happened to us three times), be taken over by the Feds, or simply stop making real estate loans.

The solution? You need an open relationship with three bankers at three different banks. That way, the lights are always on somewhere. Will this be without its own sturm und drang? Of course not—for the same reasons an open relationship has never worked for any couple since Adam and Eve: your bankers will hate it. But they will begrudgingly accept it once they understand and accept your legitimate need for a financial backup plan.

Your role then is to nurture that understanding and acceptance.

Bankers are sensitive souls. They don't get out of their offices all that often; their joys are in the neat, the orderly, and the calm. Bankers are a lot like accountants, only with personality. They love nothing better than sipping herbal tea while poring over your spreadsheets, provided, of course, your numbers are handsomely positive. They savor reports showing solid leasing and construction progress; they embrace financial statements with even the merest hint of liquidity.

While easily pleased, bankers are not perfect. They can react badly when startled. The casual mention of a second lien holder's pending foreclosure—especially one known for months—can be cause for surprising rancor. They can be oddly prickly about not having their calls returned (they have the money, after all) or about receiving a developer's reply at 6 p.m. on Christmas Eve. And bankers may be at their least charming when confronted with bold-faced lies, displaying far less in the way of patience than, say, a mental health worker. Somewhere along the line, bankers lost their childlike joy in surprises.

Bankers are aware of their senseless, pathological aversion to risk, but, knowing how unhip it is to be wimpy, they hate being reminded of it. They especially hate it when a developer tosses aside their concerns with a chuckling dismissal: "Toxics? No problem, bro. That town already glows in the dark; no one will ever notice our little spill."

The clever developer will make allowances for these personality quirks when maintaining her connection with her banker. But with a little care (under-promising is a time-honored strategy), your new best friend, your banker, will be your pal forever, or at least until he retires, gets transferred, or goes fishing.

Let Us Now Praise Famous Architects

AND LET US REMIND NOT-SO-FAMOUS DEVELOPERS to seek business counsel elsewhere.

Without a commitment to architectural innovation and excellence, without wide recognition of our best and brightest designers, our world might easily resemble the outskirts of Moscow, that endless, post-apocalyptic forest of gray, pitted concrete.

Also, let's face it, architects are always the coolest guys in the room—everybody likes them. They know the latest vacation spot (usually some islet in the Indian Ocean). They've got the hippest glasses and the best quote from the *New York Review of Books*; they're well spoken. (City councils love them.) They're urbane and witty, and they have that dash of the professorial that implies intellectual depth.

All true, but architects should come with a printed warning—perhaps as simple as tobacco's—"Warning: Architects Kill." Or more elaborately: "Warning: A design professional is like a loaded .45—take lessons before employing."

On the one hand, the marriage of a skilled developer and a top-flight architect may prove wondrous, often producing glorious offspring: a building, an entire project, swiftly designed that not only fits well with its surroundings but also is embraced by its community and is profitable from the beginning.

On the other hand, a neophyte developer or amateur owner—especially one with ego—will likely as not get his project finished, but the chances of turning a profit any more quickly than the Great Pyramids (4,500 years before becoming tourist attractions) are slim.

Why? Because, like other artists, an architect is ultimately in the business of pleasing her clients, and if a developer insists that a shopping center look like the Ponte Vecchio, the architect will design it thus, complete with a water feature that creates a moat at the center, guarding it from any would-be shoppers. Or if the developer made her first fortune in the nursery business and happens to be overly fond of landscaping, an architect will design and install a ten-foot, wrought-iron fence around his project, thereby protecting the petunias and everything else in the center from pesky visitors.

These two clownish—but true—examples (both from the Central Valley of California) illustrate the point: if you don't know what you're doing, your architect won't save you. We toured a failed mixed-use development with condominiums over ground-floor retail in Napa County that had a flaw so obviously fatal that both owner and architect should have seen it on their first visit to the dirt—it was virtually on top of a firehouse. Who would buy a home knowingly running a risk of 3:00 a.m. wake-up calls from careening fire trucks? Apparently, nobody. The condos didn't sell, and the project went back to the lender.

Yet the fault, dear Brutus, lies not in our starchitects, but in ourselves. We cannot rely on architects to tell us that second-floor retail works as often as life is spontaneously created. Or that shops facing 90 degrees away from their anchor tenant's front door are in the commercial equivalent of purgatory, just maybe a bit more dead. And we must learn the hard way what happens when we jack up our buildable area by penciling in too many compact parking spots.

As plausible as the existence of a real Lassie, there may indeed be an architect out there who will go find help if you fall down a well, but counting on either wouldn't be prudent.

Every year some cocky property owner comes to visit us, and the conversation goes like this:

McPartners: "You might consider hiring an experienced developer—developing a successful shopping center only looks easier than tic-tac-toe."

Property owner about to acquire knowledge the hard way: "Thanks, man, but we've got it covered. We have asked around, and we're hiring the best architect, the number-one engineer, blah, blah, blah—we are ready to roll. Just wanted to see if you guys would pay too much for this fabulous development opportunity."

OK, hotshot designers: Do yourselves and your inexperienced client a big favor. When you finish spinning out your ideas for the world's coolest design, advise her to seek professional development expertise. She can either hire it for a small fortune or lose a large one learning it on the job.

Developers and Contractors: General Relativity

WE TURN NOW TO CONSIDER THE GENERAL CONTRACTOR and his role in real estate. Few professions are as badly mischaracterized in our world as contractors, particularly by owners with adverse economic interests.

To some misguided developers, contractors are merely bookies with a toolbox. If a bookie takes as many bets on the Patriots as on the Steelers, the bets offset one another and the bookie keeps his juice. If a general subcontracts out 100 percent of the actual construction work—let's face it, that's what they do—and just slaps on overhead and profit, some envious developers think the contractor can't lose. The developers acknowledge the troops—in this case, the subcontractors—may get slaughtered, but they view the wily general as sitting safely behind the lines, idling at the wheel of his favorite yacht, *Change Order*.

Ignoring the thousand ways a contractor can go broke, developers all too often jump into the construction business. They forget it's not as simple as real estate's other professions: if your doodling is easier to decipher than a Rorschach test, you're an architect; if you can stack Legos at right angles, you're an engineer; if you can exaggerate convincingly, you're a broker; if you can pontificate while keeping track of your hours, you're a lawyer; and, if you can take over your father-in-law's portfolio, you're a respected developer.

They fail to consider all the talents a general must possess. Although not strictly a requirement, the conscientious general will actually know a little about construction, keeping one step ahead of the suspicious client. To instill confidence, a general must be able to stride across a muddy, obstacle-strewn construction site without seeming to care about his Gucci loafers or looking too much like a wuss when sidestepping barriers. And because they make more money at it than most touring pros, generals must be clever enough at golf to be widely considered good players yet somehow consistently lose to clients.

To succeed in this rough and tumble world, a general must speak fluent "subcontractor," a dialect in which that word that rhymes with duck is used—to the exclusion of almost all others—as subject, verb, and predicate, often in the same sentence.

Generals must know that the most important critical path in construction is the one from their own front doors to the local bank, and they will have an uncanny sense as to when to drop a change order on a client's desk. The general destined to wear the tool belt once again is likely to capitalize on the slightest mistake in the building plans. "Oh, you wanted nails with that? Where do the plans say anything about nails?"

Since there's about a pinch of truth in the foregoing, there's nothing intrinsically wrong with requiring that a contractor who has built a dozen projects for you still bid every job. It sometimes happens, however, that developers will take advantage of the inevitable frantic 11th-hour nature of the bidding process and accept a bid containing a glaring error in their favor (e.g., three bids are within nickels of one another at $10 million while one lone bid is at $8 million), figuring that, at a minimum, this will give them huge leverage during the course of construction.

For what it's worth, we have long since figured out that a contract as thick as a cornerstone won't help with a crooked or inept general and that a handshake suffices 90 percent of the time with an honest, competent one—the contract simply reminding everyone of what they agreed to do. We stopped putting our projects out to bid nearly 20 years ago, relying instead on a couple of top-flight contractors with whom we do business nearly every year, making them part of our team. Our generals work with us from day one—long before anyone knows whether a project will ever be built. They happily provide us with value engineering and cost estimating on one plan iteration after another, all without charge because they know that if the project proceeds, the work is theirs. This, we believe, is the right way to relate to general contractors.

If contractors are bookies, then we're gamblers. There's a time-honored place in the world for honest bookies, and, hopefully, for those of us gambling.

Sex, Lies, and Off-Market Deals

JESUS SPENT 40 DAYS IN THE DESERT, eating nothing and resisting the devil's temptations. Along a similar, if less biblical parallel, the IRS allows you 45 days to wander the wilderness in search of a 1031 exchange, all the while battling brokers' blandishments.

We emerged from that commercial Sahara and, while we may not have encountered the devil himself—in real estate, one can never be sure—we were sorely tempted by properties not worth a windshield inspection.

Like common wisdom, lies have a certain currency, but the more outrageous the lie, the shorter its longevity. "We're from the government, we're here to help" was so preposterous that it cannot have been uttered more than once before becoming a sad political joke. The more plausible falsehood, "It's a reverse commute," had a decent run some years back, and real estate's perennial fabrication—"This property just needs a little hands-on management"—is seldom out of play.

The Methuselah of business lies, the one that just may endure forever, has been sung by nearly every guilty chief executive: "I had no idea my employees were robbing the company blind . . . on my behalf." This absurdity coupled with the standard mea culpa—"I am guilty of trusting my team too much"—will no doubt persist until the last employee is thrown under the last bus.

Most lies, however, last only a bit longer than Christmas poinsettias no matter how much care they receive. Rapidly heading in that direction but still au courant is the claim, "It's an off-market deal." During our six weeks in the desert, we heard that more times than we could count, even with our shoes off. Apparently, never in the history of real estate had so many sellers decided that the best way to market their property was to feign indifference to its sale.

The appeal of the off-market pitch—at least to the ever-hopeful brokerage community—is that it is technically true. It is true that the off-market property isn't publicly listed for sale. What is false is usually everything else, everything the optimistic broker wishes to imply from the seller's refusal to sign a listing: namely, that the property's apparent exclusivity is the buyer's VIP pass, the chance to snare a great deal, a pirate's treasure map.

A true off-market property may indeed be a worthy prize, but brokers are seldom involved because principals deal directly with principals. Yes, it happens occasionally that an experienced owner who knows what an asset is worth will permit a broker with whom he has a longstanding relationship to quietly offer it to a buyer with whom the broker, in turn, has a similar relationship.

But that is not what one is seeing. Today's off-market deals are neither principal-to-principal nor the result of mature broker-client relationships. Rather, they are the progeny of brokers desperate for product cold-calling coy sellers. The private offering thus obtained is a lot like a Times Square Rolex—a waste of time.

If compelled to pursue a private deal, one should bear in mind that the phrase "off-market deal" is now shorthand—like "SWF" in a personals ad—for "Conniving seller seeks gullible buyer to pay 20 percent more than fair market value, pay all commissions, accept nothing as an underwriting package, and close as-is after seven days."

One might ask why any broker would bother chasing such a deal. Brokers are, by and large, at least as savvy as their clients and would surely understand the futility. Why would anyone live in Siberia? Same answer to both questions: they have no choice.

Our time in the desert revealed another unpleasant—and frankly, puzzling—development in the brokerage world: that is, the now nearly universal practice by the industry's national powerhouses to "cooperate" with outside brokers in every way except the one that matters—the commission. When a listing agent from a national firm sends his marketing package to an interested outside broker, the following conversation ensues:

"What's the split on the commission?" asks the outsider.

"No split. We keep 100 percent of the commission, but you can put yourself in for whatever you think is reasonable on top of that."

This sounds great . . . for a moment. "Wait a second. That means that if my client makes an offer that includes a 2 percent commission to me, the buyer has to pay 2 percent more than he would on a direct deal, correct?"

"Exactly."

"So my buyer is always in the hole by 2 percent compared to any one of your clients?"

"Yep."

"Once he understands that, my client will never make an offer."

The small, independent buyer-oriented brokers are thus effectively shut out of the best public deals and forced to scrounge for off-market dross.

The "we-keep-it-all" listing may be a four-bagger for the brokers, but why would any seller go along with it? Isn't it possible the small broker had the buyer with the hottest hand, the one that might actually have paid the most? How could this arrangement ever benefit a seller? Why are even sophisticated sellers willing to accept a no-share listing?

Do As I Say

THE LAST CHAPTER ENDED WITH QUESTIONS: Why would a seller ever permit a listing broker to keep 100 percent of a sales commission? Why let a broker eliminate a whole class of potential buyers: those who would never consider a property unless it was presented by her trusted outside agent? Is it not possible that an outside buyer would pay the most for the property? Random research resulted in some explanations, if not altogether satisfactory answers.

Starting with the big leagues—deals in excess of $100 million—the broker justification for keeping it all has a certain snob appeal: "There are only 200 buyers in the whole country who can do a $100 million deal and 150 of them don't have any money," explained a managing partner at one of the nation's top real estate investment banks, only half joking. "We personally know every player who can write the check. Adding an outside broker adds nothing but confusion."

But what about some unknown buyer—someone who just won the lottery or inherited $1 billion offshore? Someone controlled by a broker who will never present your deals if there's nothing in it for him? "Never happens."

But it could.

Asked if he cared whether his brokers split their commissions with outsiders, a big-league institutional seller insouciantly replied, "Nope." Why not? "I'm not worried about finding buyers in a haystack—our listings get plenty of exposure."

Maybe that works in the Bigs. But what about in Double A ball, the $5 million to $20 million range? Just as there are only about a thousand billionaires in the entire world but more than 10 million individual millionaires, there are thousands of players in the minor leagues; no single firm can have meaningful contacts with even a plurality. But that doesn't stop the nationals—hell, even the little brokers—from going for the whole commission.

The surprise is that some sellers, even sophisticated ones, permit it.

We encountered one such seller—a notoriously difficult real estate investment trust—in the $15 million sales range. According to the brokers, this seller had squeezed all the juice out of the commission in the first place—leaving nothing to share—and didn't care about (more likely, never considered) the limiting effect that approach might have on the buyer pool. Maybe that nasty maneuver works; maybe the percent or two the seller saved by screwing its own brokers offset the lost opportunity of an outside buyer.

Maybe.

A very senior brokerage executive laughed incredulously at my question, as if it were about the right cookies to leave Santa on Christmas Eve. "No one *ever* cooperates. Most agents won't even cooperate within their own firms—they hide their listings from everyone, even their own mothers. We at least force our brokers to cooperate within the company—an agent is fired immediately if he doesn't post his new listing on the company server within 24 hours. A seller always gets nationwide exposure with us."

We are all brokers of one stripe or another. We are all selling something to someone all of the time. Might it be too much to expect of any of us not born in Bethlehem to ignore the following math? A $10 million deal sold directly with a 2.5 percent commission nets the broker $250,000. Flogging the same deal farther and wider and cooperating fully with an outside broker might—just might—bump the price to $10.1 million. This would net the seller an extra $97,500 but, after splitting the commission, reduce the listing broker's commission to $126,250.

With that overwhelming financial incentive as backdrop, any knowledgeable owner should probably reject outright a broker seeking a listing who fails to ask for a keep-it-all clause. If the broker doesn't have the sense to at least ask for it, how competent can he be? It's the owner who needs to represent herself on this issue, who must understand the wide divergence of her interests and those of her broker.

If you do find yourself thinking about the right cookies for Santa or wondering whether brokers, if left to their own devices, will battle to wrest the last dollar for an owner to their own economic detriment, you might consider perusing the section on residential brokers in *Freakonomics* by Steven Levitt and Stephen Dubner. Their study of 100,000 residential brokers in the Chicago area proves statistically what we already know intuitively: brokers are best at representing themselves.

I asked that senior-most brokerage executive if he, acting as a principal, would ever sign a listing agreement in which the broker had no obligation to cooperate.

"Never."

The Back of a Napkin

IF YOU BEGIN ANALYZING SALES PACKAGES, you will soon encounter properties with numbers so flat, returns so anemic, and projections of future values so childishly optimistic that you may despair of ever finding a decent deal.

Don't.

A great deal is rarely great on the first day it is offered to you; no one consciously gives anything away in business. Because great deals are made, not born, you must analyze many properties that make little sense at their asking prices. Why? Because things have a way of changing. If his property languishes long enough on the market, a frustrated seller may become reasonable. In that hope, you underwrite his nonsensical deal today. You decide that at his $10 million asking price, the seller should be institutionalized for delusional insanity, but that at $6 million, the property might work. And then you wait. And wait. More often than not, the seller will pull his property or someone will outbid you, but if you bait enough hooks, a fish will come along.

Work listed properties, but ignore the asking prices and decide for yourself their actual values. Then follow their progress on the market, checking in with their brokers every few weeks for updates. You can, by the way, minimize luck's outsized role in hitting the seller at exactly the right moment by staying in close contact with his broker.

If being diligent and dogged in the pursuit of deals is the yin, the yang is this: if a deal doesn't work on the back of a napkin, it doesn't work. If you can't make sense of those flat numbers and anemic returns with a simple calculator, you should move on. You need only middle school arithmetic and a dash of algebra to figure out whether a deal works. If you require a quant to get you there, if you need someone to start running net present values to justify the price you want to pay today, you're cooked.

The trope "Figures don't lie and liars don't figure" is about half-right, and the right half is about half-misleading. Liars do figure. It's that most are spectacularly bad at it, only plotting a move or two in advance when ten are required. Yes, numbers are honest in their way—faithfully performing whatever mathematical gymnastics you wish—but they can, when underpinned by negligent or fraudulent assumptions, tell the most convincing lies. Figures may not lie, but their assumptions do.

Bad assumptions are myriad, but real estate has its perennial favorites. A listed property's rents will rise by, say, 5 percent a year in the future while its expenses remain fixed; a buyer will be able to terminate a below-market, long-term lease for nearly nothing; space that hasn't been occupied since the French Revolution will rent within six months after closing; and, because of the property's unique characteristics, it will outperform its overall market's vacancy and rental rates.

One false assumption seems at first blush not only benign but also reasonable—namely, that land has an intrinsic value. It doesn't. This is worth remembering well: whether raw or improved, land has no innate value. Rather, it has a cost. Even with an empty field, you reap property taxes, liability insurance, and periodic fire prevention measures. Land's only economic value is the income it receives after the costs required to produce that income are paid. If your development pro forma starts out with the seller's value for his land, you may get *there*, but likely only by accident. As likely, your equation won't work because that land value will drive your return through the floor.

Properly viewed, land value is what you are solving for with your pro forma. You could show a seller that all of the other variables in your equation—save one—are third-party, verifiable costs not subject to much negotiation. If you're going to build a project on the farmer's favorite corner, you know what your construction, financing, permit, and leasing costs will be, and you should know the rents you will achieve. The one variable subject to negotiation is the return on investment you are seeking. If, after some back and forth, the farmer ultimately concedes that your return should be fair and let's say 7 percent (I have yet to meet such a farmer), then his land value will follow automatically when you plug in the other variables in your formula. Whether the farmer himself follows is another question.

Coincidentally, this last point is a great advertisement for dealing with smart, sophisticated sellers—better yet, with developers themselves. As tough as they may be—you will never steal a property from them—they understand math and the realities of real estate development and they will ultimately acquiesce to a fair deal. Farmers, trust fund babies, and school boards do not have this understanding. Instead, they know an acre across town sold for $30 a square foot five years ago and they want $30 a square foot for their 20 acres now.

In sum, pursue deals hard, but keep them on a napkin.

No Partners, No Problems

IN THE BEGINNING, WE ALL NEED FINANCIAL PARTNERS. The wealthy may use their families and the rest of us our friends, but we start with someone else's money. As a novice, you have financial partners by necessity. Should you have them by choice later? Once you achieve a certain success, are you better off using your own money and doing fewer and smaller deals or satisfying your edifice complex with ever-larger financial partners?

It's your call. Both approaches can succeed; both can fail.

With few exceptions, the best developers in America have always had capital partners. And the arguments in favor of sticking with outside money are compelling. The first—you can do more and larger projects—needs no commentary. Deals are fun—the more, the merrier. The second is worth considering: having a financial partner is a great way to manage risk. If your partner invests 90 percent of the equity (the usual arrangement) into a partnership in which you have no personal liability, and that partnership's outside borrowing is also nonrecourse, you can make real money while having very limited risk. Say you're going to develop a project that costs $10 million and will be worth $13 million on completion, that it requires $4 million in equity, and that a bank will lend your partnership the remaining $6 million on a nonrecourse basis. Your partner puts up $3.6 million and you write a check for $400,000, a mere 4 percent of the total project cost. If the project tanks—some do—your loss is only $400,000, but truth be told, you probably charged that much in development fees during construction. Even in a loser, you're home free. And if it hits, if you sell the project for $13 million, and if you have the typical profit split with your money guy (about a net 30 percent after repayment of all capital and preferred returns), you make about a million.

If you had $4 million in the bank, you could do this single project without a financial partner and retain the $3 million profit yourself, or you could theoretically do ten projects, investing $400,000 in each, and net $10 million. This sounds so good one is reminded of the old joke about the Hollywood producer who went crazy and put his own money into a movie.

Why would anyone ever self-fund?

Because with no outside partners, you control your own destiny. You keep a property as long as you like or sell it overnight on a hunch. You avoid quarterly reports and semiannual trips to New York or Cleveland to explain the fate of your partner's money. Far more important, you avoid the risk of having someone you have never met wake up one morning and change your life by noon. Dressing in his hotel room, the pension fund chief who committed $2 billion to your financial partner hears on CNN that commercial real estate is starting to bubble. He decides on the spot to cut his exposure and tells his underlings to walk on their commitment. A few hours later, your good buddy—the vice president who until this moment acted like he ran the show— sheepishly announces that you need to either sell the project now or find a new money partner (that nonrecourse language you love in your partnership agreement works both ways—the money has no liability if it defaults). When you point out that the building is only 75 percent leased and you will both get creamed, your buddy says he understands. When you whimper that you're going to lose three years' worth of work and the chance to make millions, your former buddy apologetically hangs up.

If you were to receive this call—we did—you might decide to revise your investment strategy. You might decide that in the future you will forgo the glamour of owning a deceptively small interest in a sleek high rise and instead buy a corner gas station on your own. You might decide that having a measure of control over your life outweighs the benefits of big-time financial partners. No one from Cleveland will ever call you about your Arco. No one will insist you sell when it's lunacy to do so or, conversely, refuse to consider a sale in the hottest market ever.

You don't need a bad financial partner for problems to arise. You could have the best, kindest, most reasonable and intelligent money partner and still develop a serious conflict of interest. And it could be your fault. You and Mother Theresa could jointly decide on day one that you will hold your project for ten years. Two years later, you could be desperate—your wife dumped you, your other project went bankrupt, whatever—and need to cash out. Mother sweetly explains that a deal is a deal and that she's neither going to sell the project nor buy you out. She's content, and you are screwed.

Against this backdrop, our experience may be of some use. When we started out years ago, we had institutional money partners. Some were good, some bad—one was a downright scorpion—but they invariably, and understandably, did what was best for themselves. And if that meant crushing us like an empty can, they might have murmured the right things, but they still flattened us.

We left the financial partner world in the early 1990s, moving from large deals in joint ventures to projects a tenth the size without money partners, using our own limited capital. That decision has worked out. Over time, we have averaged a couple of projects a year and, to generate capital for our next project, we have typically sold—or better yet, 1031 exchanged—two out of three completed properties. To our mild surprise, we found we had netted as much from these small, 100 percent–owned projects as we would have in splitting profits multiple ways in big-city joint ventures. And with fewer headaches.

For what it's worth, we have consistently observed that the constraint—or bottleneck, if you will—in successful development is the lack not of capital but of quality projects. Great deals are truly few and far between. And therein lies the flaw in the assumption in the ramped-up production model just described: you cannot find ten good deals as readily as one. Rather than diversifying your risks, pushing deal quotas intensifies them.

A more accurate but less catchy title for this chapter might be "No Partners, More Control." For, as my canny Irish mother liked to say, "If you don't have any problems, you don't have any business." She may have been the worst cook in Los Angeles County, but she knew her way around running a small company.

The "NTM"

PROPERLY CONSTRUCTED, PRIMERS SHOULD be sequenced in terms of importance. The first chapter should contain the writer's best advice; the next, his second best; and so on. Turning this time-honored rule upside down, we arrive at my best advice—the "NTM."

Having read my dismissal of the IRR as little more than the bent cards of three-card monte and my questioning of the ROI's utility when used as a long-range predictive tool, the close reader may express skepticism over my unqualified endorsement of the NTM. But here you have it: if you learn nothing else from this extended epistle, learn the NTM.

The immutable laws that govern the universe are often breathtakingly elegant in their simplicity—consider Newton and Einstein—and it is thus with the first law of real estate.

What is the NTM? Rather than a formula, it is the touchstone question you should ask yourself every time you consider a deal, take a job, or enter a partnership. If asked and answered, it will detour you away from countless financial culs-de-sac.

What is it? Simply this: "the Net to Me." Phrased as a question, this is the most powerful tool in your shed. If, for example, you plumb its depths before you accept a job, you could save yourself a world of regret. Assume that potential employers offer you $150,000 a year in salary plus 10 percent of the profits in the projects they wish you to develop for them. They tell you their apartment communities cost $85 million to build and, when all goes reasonably well, sell for $100 million. The math is simple—10 percent of $15 million is a small fortune, and you're ecstatic.

But moments before you sign the employment contract, you remember this chapter and how quickly even the mightiest numbers are humbled when repeatedly divided by two. You recall the famous anecdote I mentioned about the billionaire founder of a national retail chain. This distinguished gentlemen had a penchant for young wives who refused to sign prenuptial agreements. You remember that by the time his fourth wife divorced him, his billion dollar net worth had been sliced in half four times and was down to $60 million. Remembering all this, you ask, "But what's the net to me?"

You inquire how their projects are financed, insisting on knowing how much profit actually trickles all the way to the sea. You learn that these developers have an internal money partner who funds their overhead and predevelopment costs; in return, he receives 50 percent of the net profits. You discover that the company takes on an outside financial partner for each project once it's entitled; with its preferential returns, the outside partner receives about 70 percent of the net profit. You take the $15 million profit you first envisioned and allocate 70 percent to the outside money and then half of the remainder to the inside guy. You calculate that, even if the sailing is smooth, your NTM will not be $1.5 million, but rather $225,000. You note that simply cutting the pie twice reduces your 10 percent slice to 1.5 percent.

The modest silver lining (if you're a developer at heart, you are always searching for silver linings, modest or otherwise) in having only 1.5 percent of a deal is that profits must implode before you feel it—a $1 million construction cost overrun will only sting you for $15,000.

Like Einstein, the NTM recognizes time as the fourth dimension. In the example, you solved for space—your total compensation—but, fully applied, you also solve for time, your hourly rate. If someone told Bill Gates he merely needed to cross the street to pick up that $225,000 on the curb, he would probably do it in a flash, having an hourly rate approaching infinity. If, however, your prospective employer agreed that you could have the whole $1.5 million you first envisioned, but allowed as how it might take 20 years of cankerous neighborhood meetings (we had a project take that long), you might politely decline. After a score of public hearings lasting until midnight, your hourly rate would certainly feel far less than the minimum wage.

Time is your most important dimension. In considering your NTM, solve for your hourly rate. How long is this going to take? How much of my life must I devote to this project? And, in doing so, ponder the advice a sage contractor gave a homeowner about her proposed remodel: "It will cost twice as much and take three times as long as you initially believe."

If a job offer is appealing to you, if a deal makes sense to you, if a tough listing is yours for taking, go for it, but determine your NTM first. Know where your potential income caps out, have a feel for your hourly rate, and avoid the heartache and hard feelings that inevitably accompany unpleasant financial surprises.

A salaried employee knows his NTM like his drive home from work—he sees it every two weeks on his pay stub. On the other hand, an entrepreneur, someone who risks what little capital she has and a couple years of her life on a project, should know what she can earn if the deal works out. She should be able to scribble on the back of a napkin what she stands to gain in one column and weigh it against another in which she lists what she's giving up— her salary, her medical benefits, her job security, and time with her family. Without a realistic understanding of her upside, her decision to become a developer could prove so flawed that she regrets it ever after.

Although this advice is self-evident—particularly if one is not stressing out over a job offer or a deal closing—I'm underscoring it heavily as my final point. Why? Because we have heard too many times from friends and acquaintances about how their career-launching projects were in the end bitter disappointments. Disappointments that, in our view, could have been anticipated from miles off—the profit share was suspect from the beginning—and that might have been avoided altogether by a judicious application of the NTM.

In sum, make sure the prize is worth the leap.

Best of luck.

Postscript

I SUGGESTED IN THE PREFACE that my principal theme was one of risk management, of urging you to calibrate and limit your risks—even at the cost of potential profits—as a way to weather development's storm-tossed peaks and troughs. In hindsight, a more personal and equally important theme seems to have emerged from these pages: choose your crew and fellow travelers wisely, treat them with friendship, dignity, and respect, and take the long view. A great career—and reputation—is built over decades on dozens and dozens of deals and thousands of daily decisions. While there may be no moral universe and it may sometimes appear that the unscrupulous and dishonest go unpunished in our often-hard world, you will find that, if not its own reward, fair-dealing will prove its own satisfaction.

I'm going to conclude with the thought that if you've made it this far, you will likely take the path less traveled and become a developer. I wish you the best of luck and can do no better than to repeat George Herman Ruth's immortal advice: "Never let the fear of striking out get in your way."

I would like to acknowledge a few of the many people from whom I have learned about both real estate and life. First and foremost, my wife, Michele, for everything; my partners, Beth Walter and Mike Powers, without whom my career would have surely fizzled; my dear friends Paul Gordon and Nick Farwell for their encouragement; and Vladimir Bosanac for his unwavering support of my writing. George Marcus taught me more about philanthropy than business. Much of what I learned about real estate came from listening to Jim Curtis, Bob Hughes, Dan Petrocchi, and Mark Kroll at ULI gatherings.

And from my formative years as a young lawyer desperate to be a developer, I would like to acknowledge the patient and amused guidance of Bruce Hyman, Kent Colwell, and Alexander Maisin. And finally, from my days as a bored teenager sitting on open houses for her residential brokerage business, my mother, Mary M. McNellis.

Glossary: Real Estate Jargon Demystified

WHETHER A LAWYER, ARCHITECT, ENGINEER, OR BROKER, a young professional in real estate often hears expressions—some slang, others simply arcane—that neither the finest education nor the thickest dictionary is likely to illuminate. And the professional must solemnly nod, as if understanding came with sunlight, when his client invokes acronyms and mathematical formulas to brag about the steal she made in buying a property. A combination of years deducing meaning from context and gradual insight serve to answer most questions, but some have to be asked. And asking questions one fears to be stunningly basic can prove awkward while billing hundreds an hour.

This informal guide to some of these uncommon terms will answer a few of the questions and, hopefully, spare a little of the beginner's inevitable anxiety.

Economic Terms

Capitalization rate or cap rate or simply cap (as in, "The property capped out at an 8."). A capitalization rate is a shorthand way of stating the yield a buyer would receive by purchasing a certain property. Or, to turn it around, the cap rate expresses the initial return on investment a buyer requires before buying.

Example: If you have $1 million to invest and wish to earn a 6 percent return on your investment, then you would have to buy at a 6 cap or higher. If a property is selling at a 7 cap, its buyer would receive a 7 percent return on his money. If it is selling at a 5 cap, the buyer would receive a 5 percent return, and so on.

Cap rates vary because of many factors, ranging from the attributes of the property itself (its location, vacancy rate, the creditworthiness of its tenants, the age of its roof, and so on) to the economy as a whole (interest rates, Treasury bill rates, and what product types are in favor at the moment with the buying crowd).

The mathematical formula is simple, but it's easy to trip over because the relationship between the purchase price and the cap rate is inverted. The price rises when the cap rate is lowered and falls when the cap rate is raised. The formula is this: purchase price equals net operating income (NOI) divided by cap rate (expressed as decimal).

Example: Assume NOI is $200,000. If the cap rate is 8, then the purchase price equals $2.5 million ($200,000/0.08). If the cap rate is 12, then the purchase price equals $1,666,666. Extreme examples underscore the inverse relationship between cap rate and price: if the cap rate is 1 and the NOI is still $200,000, the purchase price would be $20 million. Conversely, if the cap rate is 25, the purchase price would be $800,000.

Note: Historically, this concept was a bit more confusing to beginners because at a once-standard cap rate of 10 percent (unheard-of in the modern era), the relationship between price and cap appears to be direct: a property with $1 million in NOI sells for $10 million; a property with $100,000 in NOI sells for $1 million, and so on. This is the case only because ten is the number—and the only number—at which the teeter-totter of rising price and falling cap is exactly balanced.

Gross multiplier. Another, far simpler method for arriving at price is used in the sale of small apartment buildings. One takes the property's annual gross income and multiplies it by the agreed-on gross multiplier. If the apartments gross $90,000 a year and the gross multiplier is 12, the price will be $1.08 million ($90,000 x 12 = $1,080,000).

Internal rate of return, or IRR. The IRR is—in a perfect world—a method to determine an investor's total return from a property during his period of ownership, including both its annual cash flow and its ultimate sales proceeds. The calculation is neither simple nor without breathtaking guesswork. One takes the projected annual cash flow an investor hopes to receive from a property for a given holding period—usually ten years—and adds to that the property's estimated sale value in the tenth year. The IRR is the percentage required to discount this combined sum back to zero on the date the property is purchased.

Example: If a property produces 5 percent in annual cash flow over ten years and then sells at the end of that tenth year for twice what the investor originally paid for it, the IRR would be—trust me—10.98 percent; that is, in order to get all that cash dribbling in over the next ten years to have a net present value of zero today, you would have to discount it at 10.98 percent. Framed positively, this means you would have received a total return on your investment of 10.98 percent. Since this highly speculative 10.98 percent sounds much better than the 5 percent return you know you're getting from day one, the IRR is wildly popular.

The fallacy behind every IRR analysis ever prepared is obvious: it requires one to predict the unpredictable—cash flows years into the future and the selling price of a property ten years from now. The IRR calculation assumes one can predict highly complex and interrelated financial conditions—interest rates, capitalization rates, tenant demand, new competition, population growth, personal income shifts, and so on, long into the future. Predicting what a given property will sell for ten years hence is likely to be as accurate as predicting today how much rainfall the city in which the property is located will receive in that tenth year.

Net operating income or NOI. NOI has a widely held general meaning, but because it is the cornerstone of a property's value, its definition is subject to arm wrestling. Simply put, NOI is a property's annual gross rental income minus the property's—not the owner's—expenses attributable to the same period.

The definition of "gross rental income" has relatively few pitfalls—whether to include one-time payments (a lease termination fee) or bank interest on deposits or a tenant's repayment of over-standard tenant improvements. Sellers invariably consider tenant improvement repayments to be rent, while buyers view them as loan payments and thus not part of gross income.

The definition of "expenses" can be more problematic. For purposes of defining NOI, expenses never include the owner's debt service or depreciation. In other words, the property is viewed as being free and clear of mortgages and the tax situation is put aside. The debate begins after that: what the management fee and vacancy factor should be; whether and how much to include for reserves for future tenant improvements and leasing commissions, structural maintenance reserves, and roof replacement reserves; how to handle capital repairs or improvements; and so on.

Note to young lawyers: If possible, avoid a purchase contract in which your buyer is paying a floating price dependent on an NOI formula (this usually occurs where the sale is agreed-on before the property is fully leased). The contract has yet to be drawn that can save a buyer from being screwed by a desperate developer whose new building is failing to meet his rosy pro forma.

Architectural and Construction Terms

Alligatored. A parking lot in the midst of failure (after the first cracks but before the pot holes) is said to be alligatored. The term refers to the bumpy, cracked asphalt surface that does indeed resemble an alligator's back.

Note: A simple seal or slurry coat will not solve this problem despite whatever contrary advice your client may receive.

Bollard. A short, sturdy post used to prevent vehicle access or to protect an object (e.g., an outdoor electrical panel box) from traffic.

Clear span. A building or tenant space constructed so as to be free of interior columns. This is important in retail buildings because of merchandising requirements and sight lines.

CMB. The abbreviation for "concrete masonry block." The term describes a type of exterior wall construction. ("Is it a tilt-up?" "No, CMB. ")

Cornice. A projecting (or overhanging) continuous horizontal feature at the top of a building.

Curtain wall. The outer "skin" of an office building, usually glass, hung from a steel frame. Common construction method for high rises.

Dock high. This means that the floor of a building's loading docks are flush with a delivery truck's floor so that goods can be rolled off the truck on a level plane. This is usually accomplished by lowering the outside loading area where the trucks park.

Elevation. A drawing of a building's exterior wall viewed as if one were standing in front of it. The elevation is the stylish drawing with which the architect impresses the city council and to which the finished building sometimes bears a passing resemblance.

End cap. The space at the end of a row of shops nearest the street (hence, usually the most visible and desirable of the shop spaces).

Facade. The front of a building; the architectural treatment, hopefully impressive, of a building's principal elevation. The terms cornice and parapet tend to be used loosely (and interchangeably) as meaning the architectural treatment at the top of the facade.

Fascia. The flat portion of a building's front or principal elevation, just above the tops of the doors and windows. Also called the sign-band, the fascia is typically where building signage is placed.

Footprint. The exterior or perimeter dimensions of a building. Building footprints are typically found on site or leasing plans.

Mullion. The vertical element that separates window panes.

Note: One can roughly calculate an office's size in an office building by counting its mullions and the acoustical tile squares in its drop ceiling. Mullions are typically spaced 4 feet apart and ceiling tiles are usually either 2 feet by 4 feet or 2 feet by 2 feet.

Pad. The land area for a small building (a McDonald's) on the perimeter of a shopping center. The small building itself is also often referred to as a pad.

Parapet. A vertical wall, usually extending above a roof line. In addition to making buildings appear larger, parapets hide rooftop equipment and exterior walls (a fire wall between two buildings).

Plenum. The enclosed space between the acoustical tile ceiling (the drop ceiling) and the underside of the roof structure or, in the case of a multi-story building, the floor above.

Surveys and Plans

Surveys, site plans, leasing plans, plot plans, and so on. The when and why of these various drawings can be confusing.

Boundary survey. A formal survey prepared by a licensed surveyor of a parcel's exterior dimensions. (If not already in existence, this is the first step in developing a parcel.)

Topo. A topographic survey (the second step in the preconstruction process) is prepared by a civil engineer and details all changes in a parcel's altitudes. In other words, every hillock and declivity is calculated. This is essential for planning the parcel's site work, its drainage, and whether earth needs to be removed or imported.

Note: If a site is too low and needs earth or fill, the fill will be expensive. If, on the other hand, excess earth must be trucked away, the hauling costs will be ruinous and the dirt brokers will tell you no one is buying fill at the moment.

Geotech. A geotechnical survey (the third step in the preconstruction process) is prepared by a soils engineer and evaluates the quality and consistency of a parcel's substrata through soil borings. Knowing whether earth is predominantly sandy or claylike or rocky is critical to the building's structural design. A geotech report could kill a deal if, for example, a solid layer of granite were encountered beneath the surface.

As-built. The survey prepared by a licensed surveyor when construction is complete, showing the exact location of the buildings and site improvements (e.g., light poles and fire hydrants). The as-built serves as the basis for a subsequent ALTA (American Land Title Association) boundary survey (assuming an institution is involved). To the as-built, the ALTA adds easements, encroachments, and anything else the lender's counsel is fretting over.

Site plan. This is a less formal document, sometimes simply sketched by the project architect, showing the proposed layout of the new building and the site improvements (the parking lot and landscaping). The site plan is often, but not always, based on a boundary survey (it can be prepared from the assessor's map attached to the preliminary title report) and is used for initial presentation to planning staffs, neighbors, and so on. Typically, site plans go through numerous revisions as comments are encountered. When the size, shape, and location of the buildings are finally agreed on, the architect or civil engineer uses the site plan as the rough basis for the working drawings for the site work. The term plot plan is a less frequently used synonym.

Leasing plan. A site plan that delineates the proposed dimensions of the spaces the developer wishes to lease. The leasing plan is what developers and their brokers huddle over with potential tenants.

Tilt-up. A method of construction so common to warehouses that the buildings themselves are referred to as tilt-ups. With tilt-up construction, the form (or mold) for the exterior wall is assembled on the ground next to where the wall will stand, the concrete is poured into the form, and, when it dries, the wall is tilted up into its permanent vertical position. Because this is perhaps the cheapest means of construction, the term tilt-up is sometimes used derisively.

Truss. The wooden or metal horizontal support for a roof; the roof's understructure. Often prefabricated.

Wood frame or stick construction. Shorthand ways of referring to a building constructed of wood framing and an applied exterior, usually stucco or wood siding.

Lease Terms

Absolutely net. What a landlord strives for in a ground lease—the tenant paying absolutely all of a property's expenses.

Note: Even with an absolutely net lease, the landlord will typically have some unreimbursed expenses. For example, his partnership's tax preparation fees, the cost of excess umbrella liability insurance, and so on.

Base year. The year in which the landlord's share of a building's expenses vis-à-vis a particular tenant is established—usually the calendar year in which a lease commences or the 12-month period beginning when that tenant opens for business. In a base year lease, the tenant pays costs but only to the extent they exceed base year costs.

Note: Establishing a fair base year is tricky with new or under-leased buildings.

Definitions of Area

Because money is more important than math in the definition of a tenant's leased premises, the industry standards are subject to negotiation and one can appear foolish insisting on a particular definition as if it were an inalienable right. A Manhattan developer once said that there are more interpretations of net rentable area than languages spoken in New York.

Gross leasable area or GLA. The standard for retail leasing which, as often as not, connotes "outside wall to outside wall," meaning that the GLA is the entire building or space with no deductions. Occasionally, the measurements are from the inside—and sometimes, the midpoint—of the perimeter walls. Industrial buildings are also often leased on a gross square footage basis.

Net rentable area. This is an office leasing term and, assuming one were leasing an entire floor of a building, would be the standard for the leased premises. It is generally understood to be the total floor area less "vertical penetrations"—elevators, utility ducts, and staircases being the most readily agreed upon, while the janitor's closet and light wells are sometimes debated. Net rentable area includes all of what would be the floor's common areas if the floor contained more than one tenant—in other words, the elevator lobby, the hallways, and the rest rooms.

Net usable area. This is the calculation usually applied to multitenant floors in an office building. Net useable area is the net rentable area minus the common areas. Each tenant leases its pro rata share of the net useable area and a pro rata share of the deducted common areas; this is called a load factor. Depending on the efficiency of the floor plate (in English, the floor) and the relative bargaining strength of landlord and tenant, the load factor can vary wildly, but an average load seems to be about 10 to 12 percent. Above 15 percent, tenants scream; below 5 percent is unheard of.

Expense stop or stated expense stop. A variation to the base year approach found in office leasing in which the tenant pays the building costs over an agreed-on maximum level. For example, if the expense stop were $10 per square foot and the building expenses rose to $12, the tenant would pay $2 per square foot as its share of building expenses.

Full service or gross. A lease under which the landlord pays all costs (including janitorial and utilities) without reimbursement from the tenant.

Go dark. In retail, powerful tenants insist on the right to close their business or go dark at any time (without, however, terminating the lease or any of its other obligations). Once-burned landlords insist on the right to recapture the space if the tenant goes dark.

Industrial-gross. A typical lease format for industrial buildings wherein the tenant pays for maintenance, utilities, and increases, if any, in the landlord's taxes over those payable in the first year of the lease. The landlord pays for base year taxes and insurance.

Kick-out. In addition to a go dark provision, retail tenants often try for a kick-out clause through which they can terminate the lease upon the occurrence of some event, usually the tenant's failure to reach an agreed-on minimum level of sales.

Percentage rent. If a retail tenant is compelled to grant rent increases, all but the most successful prefer it to be in the form of percentage rent. The rate or percentage varies depending on the tenant's particular business. High sales volume, low profit margin tenants (supermarkets) typically pay no more than 1 percent in percentage rent; a discount department store may pay 2 to 3 percent while a fast-food restaurant may pay as much as 6 percent of sales or more.

Percentage rent is determined by dividing the tenant's fixed rent by the percentage rent factor (expressed as a decimal). The resulting sum is the tenant's break point or natural break point or breaker. When the tenant's annual gross sales exceed the break point, the tenant pays the landlord the agreed-on rate of percentage rent on the excess sales only.

Example: A supermarket agrees to pay $500,000 a year in fixed rent and 1 percent in percentage rent. Thus, this supermarket will pay 1 percent of its annual sales in excess of $50 million ($500,000/0.01 = $50,000,000). Put another way, it will not pay any percentage rent until its sales reach $50 million. If, for example, a Mexican restaurant agrees to pay $220,000 in fixed rent and 5 percent in percentage rent, the restaurant will then pay 5 percent of its sales but only to the extent its sales exceed $4.4 million ($220,000/0.05 = $4,400,000).

An artificial break point or breaker occurs when the parties agree that, the formula aside, percentage rent will be payable on sales above an agreed-on dollar amount. If the supermarket from the foregoing example agreed that percentage rent would commence above $40 million, then the artificial break point would be $40 million.

An observation: Because they are efficient at keeping fixed rent high, landlords rarely receive percentage rent. Typically, only very old leases or exceptionally successful tenants pay percentage rent.

Triple net. Although it is the most basic of lease terms, triple net means many things to many people. It usually means a tenant is required to pay its pro rata share of taxes, insurance, and maintenance and that the landlord is responsible for maintenance of the roof and bearing walls. The term leaves open for debate a host of lesser issues such as who pays for capital improvements or replacements (the parking lot), who pays the increase in property taxes upon the building's sale, who pays for insurance the tenant views as excessive or frivolous (a $25 million liability policy or earthquake insurance).

Loan Terms

Ammo. Slang for principal amortization or amortization schedule, as in "What's the ammo?"

Basis point. A basis point is one-hundredth (1/100) of 1 percent. For example, 25 basis points are one-quarter of 1 percent, and so on. Thus, to impress you, your client will crow about saving 100 basis points on a new loan when he might simply have said 1 percent. Basis points are often called bips.

Constant. The fixed payment of both principal and interest due under an amortizing loan, expressed as a percentage of the outstanding loan balance. In other words, the constant is determined by taking the total monthly debt service, multiplying it by 12, and then dividing that sum by the outstanding loan balance. The greater (or swifter) the principal amortization, the larger the constant. Older loans may have an attractive interest rate, but because so much of the fixed payment is principal, the cash-flow conscious buyer will object to the constant.

Example: A $1 million loan payable in 30 years with interest at 8 percent has a constant of 8.8 percent in the first year. In the 15th year of the same loan, the constant has risen to 11.5 percent (the payments are unchanged but are higher in proportion to the then-remaining loan balance of $767,700).

Debt coverage ratio or coverage. The ratio that a property's NOI bears to the annual principal and interest payments (or debt service) due under its loan. To obtain the coverage ratio for an existing loan, one simply divides the NOI by the debt service. If a property has NOI of $125,000 and debt service of $100,000, the coverage is called "1.25." If the NOI were unchanged but the debt service fell to $60,000, the coverage would be "2.08." The higher the coverage, the more conservative the loan.

To determine the maximum new loan for a property, obtain the probable lender's coverage requirement and the new loan's constant, divide the property's NOI by the coverage ratio, and then divide that result by the constant (expressed as a decimal).

Example: NOI is $327,000, the coverage is 1.15, and the constant is 8.8. Thus, ($327,000/1.15 = $284,348) /0.088 = $3,231,225 maximum loan.

Note: It is easy to forget this is a two-step process.

Leverage. A property is leveraged when it has debt on it. A 50 percent leverage means a property is encumbered with a loan for 50 percent of its value. Being completely leveraged means the owner has no cash investment in the property.

Investors love leverage because it can exponentially increase their returns. If a buyer pays $1 million all-cash for a property that then appreciates $50,000 a year in value, he makes 5 percent a year on his $1 million investment (on paper at least). If the buyer instead puts down $100,000 and borrows $900,000 from the bank, the $50,000 annual appreciation becomes a 50 percent return on his $100,000 investment. This is how the audacious become wealthy in a rising market. Turning this example on its head illustrates what happens to the audacious in a falling market. If instead of appreciating, the property depreciates by $50,000 a year, the all-cash buyer will suffer mild discomfort while the leveraged buyer will wear out kneepads in meetings with his lender.

Positive leverage. If the interest rate on the mortgage is lower than the cap rate, the buyer enjoys positive leverage.

Example: If she buys a hotel for $1 million all-cash at a 7 cap rate, she will net $70,000 a year (a 7 percent return on her $1 million investment). If rather than paying all cash she instead borrows $750,000, payable at 5 percent interest with a 30-year amortization schedule, she will pay $48,113 in annual principal and interest, but her cash investment will be reduced to $250,000. After her debt service payments, she will be left with a net cash flow of $21,886—an 8.75 percent return on her $250,000 investment. And she will benefit from annual principal amortization starting at $13,113 (and increasing yearly after that). If one counts principal amortization as part of one's return—one should—then her overall return would be 14 percent. Quite positive.

Negative leverage. This is the reverse. It occurs when the interest rate on the loan is higher than the cap rate on the purchase price. If our buyer bought that hotel at a 4 cap, the NOI of $70,000 would be unchanged, but her purchase price would have soared to $1.75 million. If the buyer has the same loan, she will still have $21,886 in net cash flow, but instead of an 8.75 percent return on investment, she will receive 2.19 percent ($21,886 cash flow/$1,000,000 equity). Buying at a 4 cap but getting 2.2 percent in cash flow is distinctly negative leverage.

Miscellaneous Terms

FF&E. A hotel term meaning "furniture, fixtures, and equipment."

Flip. A verb meaning to sell a property at the same time one is purchasing it. With a signed purchase contract and a sufficiently long escrow, a buyer of a property may, in a hot market, raise the price and secretly market it for resale before he closes escrow. The property is usually flipped (or double-escrowed or double-clutched) to the second buyer at the same moment as the flipper's purchase, with the second buyer's money the only funds in escrow. A client who indulges in this practice is a good candidate for referral elsewhere.

Rack rate. A hotel term meaning the average nightly room rental rate.